The Top
100
Dreams

The Top 100 Dreams

THE DREAMS THAT WE ALL HAVE AND WHAT THEY REALLY MEAN

IAN WALLACE

HAY HOUSE

Australia • Canada • Hong Kong • India
South Africa • United Kingdom • United States

First published and distributed in the United Kingdom by:

Hay House UK Ltd, 292B Kensal Rd, London W10 5BE. Tel.: (44) 20 8962 1230;
Fax: (44) 20 8962 1239.

Published and distributed in the United States of America by:

Hay House, Inc., PO Box 5100, Carlsbad, CA 92018-5100. Tel.: (1) 760 431 7695 or (800) 654 5126;
Fax: (1) 760 431 6948 or (800) 650 5115. www.hayhouse.com

Published and distributed in Australia by:
Hay House Australia Ltd, 18/36 Ralph St, Alexandria NSW 2015. Tel.: (61) 2 9669 4299;
Fax: (61) 2 9669 4144. www.hayhouse.com.au

Published and distributed in the Republic of South Africa by:
Hay House SA (Pty), Ltd, PO Box 990, Witkoppen 2068. Tel./Fax: (27) 11 467 8904.
www.hayhouse.co.za

Published and distributed in India by:
Hay House Publishers India, Muskaan Complex, Plot No.3, B-2, Vasant Kunj, New Delhi – 110 070.
Tel.: (91) 11 4176 1620; Fax: (91) 11 4176 1630. www.hayhouse.co.in

Distributed in Canada by:
Raincoast, 9050 Shaughnessy St, Vancouver, BC V6P 6E5.
Tel.: (1) 604 323 7100; Fax: (1) 604 323 2600

© Ian Wallace, 2011

The moral rights of the author have been asserted.

A catalogue record for this book is available from the British Library.

ISBN 978-1-84850-328-1

Printed and bound in the UK by CPI Mackays, Chatham ME5 8TD

*To Mum and Dad
for their continuing
love and inspiration*

Contents

Contents

ABOUT DREAMING

Contents

For All The Dreamers

Ever since I was a small child, I have been utterly fascinated by dreams. One of my earliest memories is having a dream about a steam train hurtling through the Scottish countryside. I was startled by the dream and, woken by my noisy commotion, my Dad came to comfort me and get me back to sleep. The next day, he took me down to stand on a bridge over the railway line and, as he held my hand, I marvelled at my dreams turning into reality, as they thundered past on the tracks below. My dad was a coal miner not a psychologist, but had an instinctive understanding of unseen patterns, and how to delve more deeply into the rich seams of possibilities.

The encouragement and guidance of my parents set me on the track to exploring my dreams and what their stories might mean. The more I studied my dreams, the more intrigued I became by the dreams of other people. Rather than just forensically deconstructing their dreams, I became fascinated by the dreamers who were actually doing the dreaming. Since those early explorations, I have had the great fortune to work with many thousands of dreamers and I would like to wholeheartedly thank them all for sharing their dreams with me.

In particular, I would like to thank those dreamers who have helped me to realize some of my dreams.

To Rhona, Colin, Matthew, Daniel and Thomas for all their love and support as I dreamt up this book and for their help in turning the dream into a reality.

To Neal Slessor for his courage and persistence in realizing his dreams and for being a true friend who is always there for me, no matter where he is in the world.

To Aileen Gibb for her constant encouragement and inspiration, and her fabulous work in connecting so many people with their own inspired futures.

To Keith Massie for sharing his journey of visionary leadership and knowing how to use a spanner to turn his dreams into the nuts and bolts of reality.

To Noel Tyl for being such a gifted psychologist and performer, and teaching me that, in order to understand the mysterious, we must first explore the mysteries of our own stories.

To Mike Powell for gracing the airwaves with his empathetic charm and opening up a different audience of dreamers for me.

To Chris Evans for his openness and generosity in inviting me to perform on his show, Helen Thomas and Suzie Dietrich for organizing it, and for all the new dream connections that have been catalysed.

Finally, to Steve Wright for being such a welcoming and enthusiastic host and bringing a wider awareness to millions of listeners every day. A big thank you also to Louise Hulland at the BBC for connecting me with Steve.

ABOUT Dreams

Ten Billion Dreams

As you read these words, one third of the world's population is asleep and by the time they awaken, they will have collectively dreamt more than ten billion dreams. The individual dreamers will perhaps have experienced their dreams as apparently random occurrences that seem to be uniquely bizarre. The vast majority of these dreams, however, will also have followed some of the familiar themes and patterns that we all experience when we dream. These dream patterns have been emerging for tens of thousands of years and form the basis for our most enduring stories and beliefs in waking life.

I have analysed more than 100,000 dreams in my 30-year career as a dream psychologist and, during that time, I have become aware that there are about 100 of these universal dream patterns that appear over and over again. Dreamers from all over the world, regardless of country or culture, report these patterns with remarkable consistency. From Russian policemen to Japanese chefs, Norwegian bikers to Venezuelan nurses, Indian dancers to Angolan oil workers, everyone, everywhere in the world, experiences these same fundamental dream patterns. These universal themes aren't just quirks of the dreaming process; they are deeper reflections of the dreamers who are actually creating the dreams.

Although we may tend to think of our dreams as being random occurrences that we have no influence over, the reverse is actually true. Dreams don't happen to us, we happen to dreams. When we dream, we effortlessly generate entire worlds, from the twinkling stars in distant constellations to the fingerprints on a lover's hand. We construct these natural patterns in our dreams because they reflect the essential nature of our waking lives. Beneath the busy bustle of our daily activities, we are trying to become more deeply aware of the true purpose and the real meaning of our lives.

The universal patterns that we create in our dreams echo this deeper search but paradoxically, it can be easy to believe that dreams are meaningless and serve no real purpose. Although our dreams may seem completely nonsensical, the key to understanding our dream language isn't just in being able to identify individual symbols but also in being able to comprehend the deeper dream patterns that we create. A solitary symbol can often seem inconsequential but it can speak volumes when woven into the richer themes of our dream stories. When we step back and look at our fundamental dream patterns, we start to see the bigger picture, both in our dreams and in our waking lives.

The 100 dreams described in this book explain the most common dream patterns that we all experience, and reveal the messages these dreams are really telling us. These patterns will be instantly recognizable to the great majority of you and provide an immediate appreciation of the individual dream meaning and message. Rather than having to identify specific symbols and then try to connect them, you can take the universal meaning of a particular dream pattern and apply it to your individual circumstances. The psychological and cultural background is also given for each individual dream pattern, and actions are suggested to help you make the most of your dream experiences.

Hopes and Aspirations

Your dreams reflect the fundamental patterns of your waking life and, although your nightly dreams and your daily life may seem to have no connection, the word *'dream'* also means your waking hopes and aspirations, as well as your night-time adventures. Even though the intentional pursuit of your waking dreams and the natural creation of your nocturnal dreams may seem to be entirely separate, they are both primarily driven by a deeper level of self-awareness that we all possess. This more elemental understanding of yourself is a natural human quality and is known as your unconscious awareness.

Unconsciousness is often equated with oblivion but your unconscious awareness is simply all the information and experience that you aren't consciously aware that you are absorbing. As a rational human being, you tend to consciously filter out most of that wider experience during your waking hours and so usually only encounter it when you dream. Although your unconscious is an area of yourself that you are often unaware of, it embodies all your past experiences and your possible futures, and can be immensely valuable in realizing your true purpose and potential in waking life.

The dreams you create are stories that express everything you are unconsciously aware of and reflect what you find most meaningful in your waking life. These stories are the natural language of your unconscious awareness and have a deeper wisdom and a broader understanding than your conscious self.

All around the world, people are unconsciously creating the same kind of stories again and again, answering questions they aren't even consciously aware that they are asking. These are often questions like *'How can I really change my life?'*, *'Why do I always fall in love with the wrong sort of person?'* or *'Why does no one recognize my talents?'*

Consistently, your dreams provide the answers to questions like these ones and, although it can be tempting to become fixated on the dream experience, there is no dream without the dreamer. You express your individual psychology through your dreams, illuminating the person you really are, what you actually need and what you truly believe. Instead of just hoping that there is some person or practice than can fix you, your unconscious awareness knows that you are already whole but are just largely unexplored. By exploring your dreams, you can become your own psychologist, guiding yourself towards fulfilment by using these insights from your unconscious awareness.

Like your nocturnal dreams, your daily life might often just seem to be a loosely connected series of random incidents that fill your days and prevent you from realizing your greatest ambitions. The pressures and demands of your waking life can leave you feeling disconnected from your bigger dreams and frustrated at your unmet needs and unfulfilled potential. By becoming more aware of your dreams, however, and how you create them to express your unconscious awareness, you can bring them into the reality of your waking life and begin to live your dreams, rather than constantly searching for them.

Shining and Searching

It can often seem that you only experience the unconscious stories of your dreams while you sleep. Every night, you immerse yourself in dream worlds that you effortlessly create, and then the alarm clock rings, urging you to step blearily into the reality of your waking life. Your dreaming, however, doesn't stop when the bell sounds because you continue to beam your unconscious awareness into the daytime spaces around you, even though you aren't consciously aware that you are doing it. As you unconsciously shine into your surroundings, your searching light illuminates all kinds of mysteries, but what is reflected back can seem complex and confusing.

You may think it is easier to ignore your unconscious expansive-ness, discarding its rich ambiguity and just focusing on what you can definitely see and are consciously aware of. Even though you try to lock out your unconscious reflections, they will continue to seep into your consciousness, giving you glimpses and fragments of your bigger picture, as if an untuned television had briefly locked onto your favourite TV show. These accidental glimpses and serendipitous fragments can often seem to convey something profoundly meaningful and it can be easy to become fixated on trying to make sense of them. The easiest and most natural way to do this is by understanding the stories that you create in your dreams.

Rather than exploring these glimpses using your instinctive dream awareness, you may try to rationalize them using your conscious mind. This rationalization can narrow your wider comprehension and it can sometimes feel like you are trying to make sense of the world by staying at home and peering out through your letterbox, instead of just opening the door and stepping outside. It may seem easier to stay inside in the apparent security of logic and objectivity but this can prevent you from stepping more fully into your dreaming awareness. Some people do step outside into their unconscious awareness, however, and use their expanded understanding to make profound discoveries about themselves and the world around them.

In 1895, Albert Einstein dreamt he was sledging down a snow-covered hillside on a beam of starlight, and used this inspiration to bring the *Theory of Relativity* out into his waking light. He later remarked that *'the gift of dreaming has meant more to me than my talent for absorbing conscious knowledge'*. By using his dream visions to expand his conscious understanding, Einstein became a true scientific visionary. Those visionaries who were open to the stories emerging from their unconscious awareness have quite literally dreamed up most of our great advances in science and technology.

Orville and Wilbur Wright used to dream about flying bicycles and realized their vision on the wind-scoured sands of Kitty Hawk, when their dreams took off in the flights of the first powered aircraft. Nobel Prize winning physicist Neils Bohr developed his model of the atom from a vivid dream in which he was sitting on the sun and all the planets were whizzing around him on separate racetracks. The organic chemist Frederich Kekulé discovered the structure of benzene in a dream, and after announcing his breakthrough he urged his fellow scientists to *'learn to dream'*.

Dream Characters

As you shine the light of your unconscious awareness into your surroundings, you aren't just sweeping randomly but are actually searching for someone who is of huge significance to you. Among all the distractions and ambiguities, you are looking for reflections of yourself as you try to understand who you truly are. Your true identity rarely reveals itself in a random sweep of awareness, however, and so you are instinctively drawn to situations that reflect your character. The best mirrors for your self-awareness are other people and, by unconsciously absorbing what they reflect back, you often become more enlightened about your character.

Although it may seem more logical to think of yourself as a single identity, as described by a passport or security badge, every individual accommodates a unique family of characters. Your different characteristics appear at different times, depending on what you are doing and where you are. Sometimes, the characters you embody may seem to be quite routine and so, as your day starts, you might find yourself showing up as a spouse, then a parent, and then stepping into your professional identity as you enter your workplace. At other times, your characteristic behaviour may seem quite unfamiliar and you hear yourself saying things like *'I don't know what possessed me to do that'* or *'I just wasn't feeling myself'*.

You may try to consciously ignore your different identities in your waking life but they will continue to reveal themselves in your dreams. The characters that you create in your dreams are aspects of yourself and you construct them from your experiences of people who embody those characteristic qualities. If you don't know anyone who has the particular characteristics that you want to express, then you just make someone up, using a combination of character nuances you have unconsciously observed in other people. These original characters can often guide your understanding of a situation that you can't comprehend consciously.

The behaviour of your dream characters usually reflects your relationship to these particular aspects of your character. For example, when you dream of a loved one, you are reflecting on the deeper and unspoken qualities of your character. In any close loving relationship, it can sometimes be difficult to distinguish where your identity ends and the identity of your partner begins. If you are separated from them for any length of time, it may feel as if part of you is actually missing. The loved ones in your dreams help you to understand what this person really means to you and how they can enrich and inspire your daily life.

Some of the most frequently occurring characters in your dreams may be public figures and celebrities. Although you might not have spent time with them in real life, you may feel you know them intimately by their public appearances and from media reports of their life events. Celebrities usually symbolize particular talents and achievements, and their appearance in your dreams can often awaken you to valuable and unique aspects of your character that are just waiting to be discovered. Even before the advent of televised talent shows, our ancestors used a whole range of gods and goddesses to characterize unique talents and abilities

Dream Animals

As well as generating all the human characters that inhabit your dreams, you also create all the creatures encountered in your nightly adventures. Your dream animals represent your more instinctive nature and, although we humans may like to consider ourselves as a higher form of life, we still live in animal bodies, with natural instincts and intuitive impulses that sometimes seem inappropriate and impolite in waking life.

Even though your instinctive nature may appear dangerous and uncontrollable, the animals in your dreams usually hold a creative and innate wisdom, which can be difficult to consciously access in day-to-day situations.

Our dream animals reflect our unspoken power, and some of the first recorded dreams of our ancestors are found in the 30,000-year-old animal paintings in the cave of Chauvet-Pont-d'Arc in the Ardèche region of southern France. Almost all human cultures have beliefs around the characteristic powers of particular animals, such as the cat gods of the ancient Egyptians and the totemic dream animals of the Native American Indians. In many societies, these animal powers are still used by shamans as a way to connect with a heightened intuitive awareness, as they mediate between the realms of the conscious and unconscious.

We create a whole range of animals in our dreams, from threatening scary monsters to loyal domestic pets. Household pets reflect the parts of your instinctive nature that you feel comfortable with, while wild animals reveal parts of yourself that you want to understand, even though it seems that they may never be tamed. Although we may not consciously follow shamanic traditions, we stay close to our animal spirits by nurturing our domesticated animals, giving them human names and treating them as respected members of the family. As children, we often associate our pets with all sorts of magical qualities and some of our best-loved companions are animal totems in the form of teddy bears and other cuddly toys.

The first stories we hear and read in our childhood are almost entirely populated by animals, and animal noises are some of the earliest sounds we make, as we unconsciously express our

instinctive animal qualities. Beyond our meowing and mooing, we start to identify with characters in cartoons, of which many are talking animals. We continue to connect with our innate animal nature in our dreams, creating fantastic animals that can talk, some of which seem to be part animal and part human. These fabulous creatures often take on a life beyond our dreams, appearing in our myths and stories in such forms as sphinxes, werewolves, or Winnie the Pooh.

Although we can feel under social pressure to tame our natural instincts, suppressing our animal natures can cause us to feel stressed and ill at ease. The animals encountered in our dreams can often show us where our physical bodies are in need of nurturing and attention. Like the shamans, most healing traditions use animals to represent their healing powers. Even those who rigorously practice western medicine represent themselves by the entwined snake wrapped around the Rod of Asclepius. No matter how much we try to repress our instincts, our dream animals will always be there, soaring and prowling in our unconscious awareness, inspiring and empowering us.

Dream Events

The characters and creatures you encounter in your dreams also generate most of the action and you experience these dramas as your dream unfolds in a series of events. One of the most common phrases used by dreamers, when describing a dream, is *'and then'*, usually in the form of a whole series of *'and thens'* until the final *'and then I woke up!'* These *'and thens'* mark the significant events in your dream and help shape how you develop it into your dream story. As you connect with the other characters during these events, your unconscious characteristics are developing the plot of your individual story.

Although it may seem as if every series of dream events is unique, they usually follow similar themes. These universal events that we experience in dreams have formed the plots for some of our most powerful myths and stories in waking life. Joseph Campbell, the American mythologist who inspired George Lucas to create *Star Wars*, studied thousands of dream-driven myths from hundreds of cultures around the world and found the same event structures enacted in almost every myth. These mythological event structures resonate deeply with us because they so powerfully reflect our individual life stories.

The three fundamental events in our dreams and stories unfold in the sequence of answering a call to action, then making a decisive and deepening commitment, finally followed by a triumphal realization of our inner gifts. Like all the great stories we tell in literature, we usually enter a dream just before the call to action. In a stage play, this would be Act I, or what a Hollywood screenwriter would call the set-up, with a bit of backstory. The call to action leads into Act II, which is usually the main part of the story. As we venture deeper into the drama, we have to make a difficult decision, marking the middle of Act II.

We often run away at the decisive moment but if we do choose to make a deeper commitment to ourselves, we find ourselves travelling further into Act II and being faced with even more challenges. As we rise to meet these new challenges, we break through into Act III, where we finally resolve the dramatic tension that originally called us into action. As the curtains close or the credits roll, we realize that the story has given us a much profounder awareness of our gifts, both in our dreams and in waking life. This sequence of dream events can be found in almost every classic play or film.

A typical dream episode lasts between 15 and 45 minutes but you can pack whole lifetimes into these time frames by only acting out the parts of the dream that actually propel the story along. Like a supremely skilled screenwriter, you automatically keep the action moving and the events unfolding so you can continue to reveal the motives and desires of the characters that you are creating. It may appear as if you dream in real time but you actually dream in story time, fragmenting and compressing your dream narratives, as you focus on the most significant events in your stories.

Dream Places

Your dream characters act out the events of your stories in a boundless variety of dream places that you create for them. These dream landscapes mirror your inner world, reflecting where you feel you are at in your waking life. Familiar dream places usually evoke a particular locality that holds special memories for you, such as a childhood home or a classroom. As well as revisiting these familiar locations, you also create unfamiliar places so you can explore unknown possibilities and potentials that may be emerging in your waking life. As you make your way through your dream places, you are exploring ways of getting to where you want to go in your life.

When you dream of being inside a building, such as a house or an office, then you are examining your character and the potential that you know you embody. Dreaming of being outside means you are considering what lies beyond your immediate awareness and how you can investigate those possibilities. Urban locations, such as towns and cities, represent the complex knowledge and rich experience that you have been building up in your waking life. Rural locations and wild places are evoking your more expansive and opportunistic nature. Travelling to distant lands in your dreams shows you are encountering something that may seem foreign in your daily life.

The language we use in everyday life echoes our unconscious awareness of our inner landscapes. We talk about making a great effort as *'having a mountain to climb'*, which may end in a real *'cliffhanger'* of a situation. When we get fixated on minor details and find it difficult to see the wider perspective, we say that *'we can't see the wood for the trees'*. Even though we may live miles from the sea, we may hear ourselves asking if *'the coast is clear'*. When working with something familiar, we say we feel *'really at home with it'* or *'it's right up my street'*.

As you shine your unconscious awareness out into your surroundings in waking life, you sometimes find locations in the outside world that seem to resonate with your inner landscape. This can often give you a feeling of deep connection with a particular physical location that may become an extremely inspiring place for you. Certain locations can reflect the inner worlds of whole groups of people and, over time, these sites evolve into mythical places that are regarded by many as being vital to their inner life. Some people might build temples and shrines to celebrate these sacred spots, while other groups may congregate in the sports grounds that surround their hallowed turf.

Your unconscious awareness of who you really are is deeply rooted in an appreciation of where you have come from and an understanding of where you are going. All our cultures have otherworldly promised lands and dream places, known by names such as Shangri-La, Shambhala, Hyperborea and

Utopia. As you watch other people sitting at a desk or walking down the street, you can often glimpse a distant look in their eyes, as their unconscious awareness roams freely in their dream places. These dream destinations may not exist in an atlas or have GPS coordinates but they are very real places in our unconscious landscapes, places where we can truly be ourselves.

Dream Objects

As well as the characters, events and places you create, you also make all the objects in your dreams. Your dream objects reflect the tools and resources you have available to shape your waking life and, like the rest of your dream world, these dream objects have a deeper significance that goes beyond their ordinary utility. Your dream objects become imbued with a meaning beyond their physical qualities and become items with almost magical properties. The object itself isn't really magical, however, as it is only reflecting your innate talents as you shine your unconscious awareness on to it.

For tens of thousands of years we have been trying to make sense of what these objects unconsciously reflect back to us in our dreams and waking lives. We often try to do this by logically examining our unconscious reflections but this can often lose much of the meaning that we sense at a more instinctive level. It is difficult to describe the seemingly irrational using only rational language and so, in all our cultures and all our creeds, we have evolved symbols as a way to try and objectively define the indefinable. A symbol is a tangible representation of an intangible meaning that can't be fully expressed by our conscious awareness.

Dream objects acquire their symbolic value through the unconscious awareness of meaning that they evoke in us. Symbols may seem like an abstract concept but they surround us everywhere, from corporate logos to computer icons, from team colours to religious iconography. Our ancestors communicated using symbols before they developed speech and, even after the evolution of all our spoken languages, we continue to use symbolic imagery to articulate our deepest feelings. We use these dream objects to express what we can't put into words and our symbols aren't just a substitution for something else, they are a way of connecting us to something beyond ourselves.

The word *'symbol'* comes from the Greek word *symbolon,* which was a token, often a coin or a bone, which was broken in two, with each half being given separately to two people. These two people could then validate each other's identity by checking that their tokens fitted together perfectly. This was a way of establishing trust and connecting authentically with someone beyond their familiar acquaintances. Having this property of being able to connect someone with something beyond themselves gives the symbol its meaning and is what makes it so valuable, rather than it having any intrinsic physical value.

In our modern waking lives, the objects that connect us with something beyond ourselves are the ones that we ascribe with most symbolic value. These may be symbols of our beliefs or faith but the dream objects we currently tend to value most are the mobile phones we use to communicate with other people beyond ourselves. Our phones have the potential to connect us with a bigger sense of self and it is why they have become such ubiquitous and necessary objects. Our dream objects are also unconsciously connecting us to something more meaningful beyond ourselves, and our human nature means we can't help but to explore those connections.

Dream Language

The imagery and symbols we create in our dreams convey us beyond our selves and also help us to convey our dream experiences as we express them to other people. The Ancient Greeks provided us with the word *'metaphor',* which means to convey some quality from one thing to another. The Greek philosopher and playwright Aristotle, who observed that *'The most skilful interpreters of dreams are they who have the faculty of observing resemblances',* noted this metaphoric ability of our dreams to connect and transfer meaning. Another Greek scholar, Artemidorus, the author of *Oneirocritica*, the first modern dream dictionary, said *'Dream interpretation is nothing other than the juxtaposition of similarities'*.

Metaphor is the native tongue of our imaginal realms and, although we all speak it, it can sometimes seem like a foreign language learned in school but somehow forgotten. We often find ourselves, however, unconsciously speaking the metaphors of our dream language in the idioms we use in everyday speech. Although it seems instinctively natural to say *'under the weather', 'a piece of cake', 'all in the same boat'* or *'water under the bridge',* these figures of speech only appear strange when you think about what you have actually just said.

The idiomatic imagery we use in our dream language isn't just random but describes our metaphorical dreamscapes. We use the solidity of land to represent practicalities and realities, using language like *'down to earth', 'solid effort'* and *'well grounded'*. Often the sky symbolizes thought and ideas with phrases such as *'blue-sky thinking'*, *'airing your views'* and *'shooting the breeze'*. Water symbolizes emotions and experiences with words like *'feel it in my water'*, *'floods of tears'*, and *'at a low ebb'*. Fire and light represent creativity and passion with terms such as *'burning desire'*, *'all fired up'* and *'a light-bulb moment'*.

Even as spoken and written languages evolved, we began to turn our words back into images so we could express an even deeper meaning when we dream. Our dreams often speak using puns when we see a valuable image that coins a phrase for us. These dream puns use two words that sound the same but have different meanings, and are known as homophones. For example, many celebrities have reported dreaming about appearing in a film with the actress Faye Dunaway. This was not mere wish fulfilment but an ongoing anxiety that their career was in decline and their celebrity status would soon be *fading away.*

Most cultures have stories telling of a single unified human tongue that existed prior to the wide diversities of our current spoken and written human languages. One of the best known of these accounts describes the Tower of Babel where all humanity could converse in a single language, before they were scattered to all corners of the world where they developed into separate languages. Regardless of how much truth there might be in the tale, the universal human language still continues in the visual imagery of our dream symbols and metaphors. Every time you use an idiom or metaphor in waking life, you are speaking in the instinctive language of your dreams.

Dream Stories

We instinctively use the language of imagery as we create our dreams, and we find ourselves naturally building up our symbols into more complex patterns. These patterns are the primary devices that we use to explain our world and understand ourselves, and we call them stories. If we don't understand something in waking life, we try and find some meaningful themes in the situation and then relate these patterns to each other as stories. When we enquire about the complexities of a situation, we will usually ask *'What's the story?'* and if we feel that the patterns we see are becoming disjointed and meaningless, we often say we have *'lost the plot'*.

It can sometimes seem as if our dreams are somewhat fleeting and illusory but most of the world's great and enduring works of literature have been inspired by their author's explorations of their unconscious awareness. James Joyce was one of Ireland's most gifted storytellers and although his favoured style has been termed *'stream of consciousness'*, it could be described more accurately as *'stream of unconsciousness'*. One of Joyce's most famous novels, *Ulysses*, is an unconscious stream of imagery set in a formal mythic pattern, based on the dreamlike journey taken by Odysseus in Homer's epic poem *The Odyssey*. Joyce continued to share his stream of unconsciousness with even more dream imagery and homophones in *Finnegan's Wake*.

Another of our greatest storytellers, the playwright and poet William Shakespeare, regularly used his dreams as the foundation for the eloquent brilliance of his dramas. Many of Shakespeare's plays appear to be dream dramatisations, starting with the dreams and omens in his early histories such as *Henry VI* and *Richard III*, and continuing in his use of dream imagery in the dagger scene in *Macbeth*, and in Juliet's life-giving kiss to Romeo. As well as using dreams as the foundations for his plots, many of Shakespeare's plays have dreamlike settings, such as the Bohemian forest in *A Winter's Tale*, Prospero's enchanted island in *The Tempest* and the dreamy world of *A Midsummer Night's Dream*.

William Shakespeare and James Joyce are lauded as literary giants but in our dreams we are all world-class writers and playwrights. Our dreams are like an involuntary poetry that doesn't just describe a space but uses metaphorical imagery to creatively construct it. The stories we create in our dreams are always trying to connect us with something beyond ourselves by transferring a deeper meaning from our inner life out into our outer waking life. As we build up meaningful patterns, by connecting the fragments of our experiences, our unconscious awareness articulately expresses the bigger stories of our lives.

Like our dream patterns, the stories we tell in waking life are also based on a number of fundamental patterns. Our most powerful modern stories are often unconscious retellings of enduring older tales. Steven Spielberg's *Jaws*, based on a novel by Peter Benchley, bears an uncanny and unwitting resemblance to the 1,200-year-old tale of *Beowulf*, an Old English heroic epic poem, which takes place in the coastal town of Heorot that is being menaced by the water monster Grendel. Our dream stories directly connect our waking reality to stories from the greater reality that forms the foundation for all our art, psychology, spirituality and mythology.

Dream Mythology

In our modern world, a myth is usually considered to be an unsubstantiated or irrelevant belief. We might say something is *'just a myth'* or *'just a dream'* but, in so doing, we disconnect ourselves from our own bigger stories. Our myths aren't just insubstantial stories but form a much deeper framework that

we use as a way of making meaning and understanding our lives. It can often seem as if ancient myths aren't relevant in our contemporary cultures, but the myths we have created since we started sharing stories are our most fundamental form of psychological exploration.

The stories originating in ancient mythologies form the foundations for all our modern psychology and behavioural investigation. Although myths may appear to be all about gods and goddesses – usually involving fantastic creatures and unlikely events – they actually describe fundamental patterns of human behaviour. Even though a specific myth might seem to describe a particular event, it also tells a story about a universal human experience. These patterns, which are told and retold in myths, are also the same patterns that you illuminate and connect with in your unconscious awareness. We use these mythical patterns to connect ourselves to the bigger picture and find a sense of perspective and meaning in our lives.

It may seem as if mythology is just ancient stories from days gone by but our modern lives are alive with contemporary myths and legends. From the daily dramas of soap operas to sweeping cinematic extravaganzas, the mythical foundations of our fundamental human behaviours surround us. We use much of our storytelling culture, from the simplicity of fairy tales to the complexity of Arthurian epics, as a way of incorporating these basic behavioural patterns into our individual stories. Our personal mythology helps us to naturally understand patterns that are difficult to make sense of rationally, and encourages us to step into the unknown, going beyond the boundaries of what we know.

As dogmatic scientific thinking and organized religions have evolved and grown, we have become more and more disconnected from our personal mythologies. Like our dreams, however, our myths are creative works that allow us to transcend the limitations of rational thought and use our imagination to its fullest extent. Understanding that myths aren't accounts of actual events, but are actually behavioural templates, means we can use them to support and explore our imaginative powers. Our individual dreaming performs the same function as collective mythologies but at a private and personal level it helps us to truly recognize the richness and complexity of our personal stories.

Becoming aware of your individual mythology enables you to become more aware of the different characters and identities you play out in the dramas of your daily life. Your mythology helps you to orient yourself, to understand where you are and realize where you are going as you travel through life on your personal quest. For a human being, having a mythical life is as important as having a physical life, as your individual mythology forms much of the unseen framework that you live your waking life within. Our dreams are our individual myths and our myths are our collective dreams.

Dream Psychology

When exploring dreams, it can be all too easy to become fixated on the dream and find yourself ignoring the dreamer who is creating all the dreams. To really understand the meanings and messages from the dreams, it is incredibly helpful to have an understanding of the dreamer and their potential behaviour patterns. Psychology is the study of human behaviour and goes beyond the purely conscious and physical manifestations of what it means to be human. Although psychological studies can be complex explorations with many apparent contradictions, the basics of psychology are *who you are, what you need* and *what you believe*.

Who you are is usually revealed by the identities of the characters you create in your dreams. From a psychological perspective, identity is always associated with action, so the more aware you are of your characteristics, the more easily you will find it to achieve your ambitions in waking life. As well as the characters you create, dreams reflecting who you are usually involve some sort of decisive choice. Identity dreams often also contain buildings, which represent yourself and others, and may feature barriers and obstacles, which symbolize your personal boundaries. By acknowledging your various identities, it is usually much easier to come to the right decision and follow the best course of action.

What you need is often shown by what seems to be most valuable and significant in your dream stories. Your needs are usually reflected in what you value most, so whatever you keep being drawn towards in your dreams indicates where your values lie in waking life. Dreams showing what you need are often signified by the discovery of treasure or the loss of something valuable. Your needs are also expressed in dreams where you are creating something or trying to get rid of something, and also in adventures of love, intimacy and desire. Dreams filled with surprises and unexpected breakthroughs can also show what you really need.

What you believe is your particular viewpoint as you look at a specific situation. As you unconsciously search for your identities and gravitate towards what you value, you find yourself on a journey that transports you through a variety of different viewpoints and perspectives. Dreams voicing your beliefs often involve communicating in some way or being unable to say what you really want. Belief dreams can also involve searching for something but never finding exactly the right thing. Dreams where you travel by exploring possibilities are also about what you believe, as is any dream where there is a sense of mystery or transcendence.

In *The Top 100 Dreams*, you can see these basic patterns of human psychology emerging again and again in the dream stories that we all create. Recognizing these fundamental themes can help you to become more clearly aware of your identities, needs, and beliefs. The more you are aware of *who you really are*, *what you actually need*, and *what you truly believe*, the easier it will be for you to make decisions, attract value, and really express yourself. Your dreams, however, aren't just some abstract psychological theories but vibrant meaningful stories that make most sense when you step into them and find out what they really mean.

THE TOP 100
Dreams

1. BEING CHASED

Dream

You find yourself being pursued by someone or something that you feel is going to harm you in some way. There may be more than one individual chasing you, or perhaps an animal or a monster. You are constantly running and hiding and trying to stay ahead of whatever is pursuing you. There seems to be a continual threat of attack and injury but no matter how fast you run, you can't ever reach a safe and secure place. It seems impossible to escape from whatever is pursuing you and you become more and more anxious with every step.

Meaning

Although you would normally find it easy to escape from your pursuer in waking life, you just can't escape from them in this dream. No matter how fast you run or how expertly you manage to conceal yourself, they are always there with you. This is because whatever is chasing you is always some aspect of yourself and wherever you go, there you are. This particular aspect of your behaviour is something that you only experience in certain situations in daily life and is usually triggered by a specific event or a particular person. It isn't the event or person, however, that is actually chasing you; it is how you perceive that person or situation and what that reflects in your own character.

The form that the pursuer takes will reveal what aspect of yourself this actually is. Being chased by an animal indicates there is an instinctive impulse that you are finding hard to contain in waking life. When a monster is pursuing you, it reflects that you have a raw and powerful talent but are finding it challenging to evolve and refine it. If a man, woman or a gang is chasing you, then you have the opportunity to assert a particular talent but may be running away from some of the responsibilities involved in displaying your abilities. Although they seem scary, your pursuers are actually bringing your attention to unrealized powers and talents in your pursuit of fulfilment.

Action

The way forward from this dream is to connect and engage with whatever is causing you to experience this ongoing tension in your waking life. This will usually involve stepping outside your comfort zone and taking assertive and confident action to resolve the situation and move on. It can seem easier and more comfortable to avoid doing anything but this usually causes the tension to build up even more. Confronting the issue enables you to stop feeling like a helpless victim and enables you to confidently direct the outcome to your advantage. Rather than being pursued, you become the one pursuing your chosen opportunity.

Background

Our modern society still reflects behavioural patterns that emerged from our hunting and gathering activities during the Stone Age. During that time, we were either chasing something because we wanted to eat it, or escaping from it because it wanted to eat us. Even though the opportunities we chase in modern society tend to be less dangerous, we still term any

activity that is meaningful for us as a pursuit. The goals we pursue form the basis of all our hopes and aspirations and these are most clearly expressed in our dreams, whether we are asleep or awake.

2. TEETH FALLING OUT

Dream

Everything seems fine until you suddenly notice that some of your teeth are becoming loose and starting to fall out of your gums. You desperately hope that your other teeth are still intact but then they start to wobble too. It may be that you end up spitting out your teeth as your mouth fills up with blood, or perhaps your teeth just crumble into powder. You might also find yourself looking in the mirror and realizing that your teeth are badly decayed, or you have somehow grown fangs like an animal or a vampire.

Meaning

When you dream about your teeth, you are usually considering how confident and powerful you feel in waking life. You show your teeth when you smile and when you bite, and so they often reflect how self-assured and assertive you are feeling. Losing your teeth indicates something is challenging you and causing you to lose confidence in your ability to deal with it. Like teeth dropping out one by one, receiving a knock to your confidence in one area of your life can often cause you to lose nerve in other areas of your life. Your self-assurance begins to wobble and you often find it easier to just to keep your mouth shut rather than speaking up for yourself.

Crumbling teeth show that your confidence is being eroded because you aren't taking care of your self-esteem and if your teeth are decaying, then you feel that your power is somehow fading away. A loose filling suggests you are no longer filled with confidence and bleeding tooth sockets indicates tension in a close relationship is somehow wounding your self-esteem and you are letting your self-worth just leak away. If you are wearing a brace, then you are trying to maintain your confidence using external support. Gleaming veneers and crowns suggest you are putting on an artificial show of power. Vampire teeth and fangs indicate you may be relying on the energy and passion of other people to provide your self-assurance.

Action

The message from this dream is that you should be more confident in whatever situation is currently challenging you in your waking life. Although you may feel powerless in the face of adversity, you can often change the balance of power by just acting in a more self-assured manner. The more confident that you appear then the more likely you are to succeed in overcoming any difficulties. Rather than seeing the unknown and uncertain as something that will leave you powerless, relish it as a challenge you can really get your teeth into.

Background

We all experience our teeth actually falling out when we lose our deciduous, or baby, teeth as children. During the period when our teeth fall out we are usually starting to negotiate power and identity in our relationships with others. It often seems, however, like everyone else, such as our parents and our teachers, have all the power and we are relatively powerless. As a child, this can cause us to lose self-assurance and when we experience this loss of confidence in adult life, we often dream that our teeth are falling out again.

3. UNABLE TO FIND A TOILET

Dream

You are desperate for the toilet and you are searching frantically to find one. The only toilets you can find, however, are in strange places or in full public view. The cubicles may have no walls or a door that you can't lock. You might also find yourself in a queue and, even though you urgently need the toilet, have to wait in line. When you actually reach the toilet, it is often disgustingly messy and cramped, or flooded and blocked. You worry about getting your shoes wet and there is usually no toilet paper or place to wash your hands.

Meaning

In waking life, the toilet is where you go to release what is no longer healthy or sustaining for you. Dreaming about needing the toilet indicates that there is some situation in your life that has become unhealthy but you aren't sure how to let go of it. This often involves your personal needs and how easily you find it to express them to other people. Searching for a toilet shows you are looking for some way to tell someone what you really need. This can feel strange for you, however, and the need for privacy shows you would like to deal with this situation behind closed doors, so that you don't appear needy. Having to stand in a queue for the toilet indicates that you are putting the needs of others before your own, even though you are desperate to express them.

You are anxious it will turn into a messy situation if you try and voice your needs. This cramps your self-expression because you feel you have little choice and no room to manoeuvre. You are also worried that it might end up becoming very emotional with floods of tears or that your requests for help may be blocked. Trying not to get your feet wet indicates that you are over-cautious about stepping into emotional situations because you are unsure what the outcome might be. Sometimes you just want to come clean and wash your hands of the whole affair but there seems to be no way for you to do this.

Action

In waking life, you often hope your needs will be met if you look after other people's needs, but they often seem to just end up dumping their problems on you. The best way to resolve this situation is to put your needs before the needs of others by using the word *'No'* now and again. This enables you to set firm personal boundaries, which allow you to look after your needs. Although this may seem selfish, it is much easier to look after other people's needs when you are comfortable that you can attend to your own.

Background

Our first experience of controlling our needs happens at a very young age when we learn to regulate our basic bodily activities in toilet training. This is often our first exposure to

social obligations taking precedence over our physical needs and functions. During this training, we realize that inappropriate expression of our needs can become very messy and also can make us feel quite ashamed. Even though we learn to control our physical needs as children, we often find it challenging to manage our emotional needs as adults as they can evoke the same feelings of vulnerability and embarrassment.

4. NAKED IN PUBLIC

Dream

You are surprised to find yourself completely naked in a public place and are making frantic attempts to shield your body or hide behind whatever cover you can find. Everyone else around you is fully dressed and, even though you are extremely embarrassed, no one else seems to notice your nudity. You are more concerned about people seeing you naked than being cold or physically uncomfortable. Although you may not be entirely naked, you may have a vital piece of clothing missing, revealing your naked skin for all to see. It may be that you are only naked from the waist down or perhaps wearing a jacket but no shirt.

Meaning

When you dream about being naked in public, there is some situation in your waking life making you feel vulnerable and exposed. People who are entering an unfamiliar situation, such as a new job or relationship where they feel that they lack confidence in their abilities, often experience this dream. The clothes you wear represent the image that you feel comfortable showing to the world. They form a protective barrier that helps you to conceal your true self when dealing with other people. Although you are happy to completely open up in private, it can make you feel very uncomfortable if you can't cover up the more personal areas of your life in public.

Even though you try and hide your discomfort by whatever means you can, no one else seems to notice because you still appear secure and confident to them, rather than the exposed and vulnerable person that you feel. Your concern about showing your vulnerability may make you appear cold towards other people in your daily life, and hiding your true feelings may make them feel uncomfortable. If you are missing a vital piece of clothing, it suggests that you are usually confident but feel that you have a chink in your armour. The more you cover yourself up, however, the more difficult it is to display your unique gifts. There are often situations in your life where the only way to truly express your talent is just to open up and be your authentic self.

Action

This dream is helping you to uncover your need to express your talents. It can seem easier to hide your abilities away so that they won't be exposed to the judgements and criticisms of other people. Although this can seem the safest thing to do, it can lead you to feelings of frustration and disappointment. By choosing to keep your gifts under wraps, you constantly have to show up as other people expect you to appear, rather than showing up in a way that really suits you. The more you reveal your talents to other people, the more you find out about your uniqueness.

Background

Our skin forms the visible boundary between our inner and outer lives, and we can sometimes feel vulnerable when that boundary seems unguarded. We often use the terms *'thick skinned'* or *'thin skinned'* to describe how someone copes when they are exposed to criticism or abuse. Exposing flesh in public is far more accepted now in many cultures than it used to be and we are surrounded by images of scantily clad people in the media. Even those people who choose to bare their skin in public, however, often use a tattoo as an assertion of identity and a barrier against vulnerability.

5. UNPREPARED FOR AN EXAM

Dream

You arrive to sit an important formal examination but are shocked to realize that you have done absolutely no studying. You knew about the exam well beforehand and had plenty of time to revise and prepare for this moment. For some reason, however, you haven't done any preparation and now it is far too late to do anything about it. You are really disappointed with yourself because you know this is a very important test and a poor result will reflect badly on you. This inevitable failure will prevent you from following some ambitions that you really want to pursue.

Meaning

Dreaming of being unprepared for an exam often indicates that you are critically examining your performance in waking life. You have set yourself some standards in daily life that you think you need to achieve in order to be truly recognized and appreciated by other people. If you feel that you aren't managing to live up to these standards, however, then you will feel that you have failed in some way. Although it may seem like an external authority is setting the exam, it is you who is setting the criteria for whether you pass or fail. You feel unready for this critical period of self-examination because your level of self-awareness isn't as deep as you would really like it to be.

Your feeling of being unprepared often arises because you tend to leave nothing to chance in your waking life. You usually prepare meticulously for any task that you have to do, whether it is a major project or a trivial errand. This can lead to expecting far too much from your performance and creates a constant anxiety that you will end up with a poor result. Although this tension drives you on and gives you an enviable record of consistent success, it can also result in you neglecting some of your more fundamental needs. The real criteria for success isn't whether you achieve a certain level of competence but how much you know about what makes you really happy and fulfilled in life.

Action

The best way to successfully move on from this dream is to consider what makes you happiest and most fulfilled in life, and how successful you are in achieving it. This is often something joyous and spontaneous, which doesn't require endless preparation. When you judge yourself too harshly, you will always feel like a failure, no matter how brilliantly successful

you might actually be in waking life. Rather than immersing yourself in endless self-examination, the real test of your character is being able to accept your talents by celebrating your knowledge and achievements, instead of constantly judging them.

Background

Examinations are how we are judged according to the expectations of others and they reflect how we judge ourselves according to our expectations. Although formal academic testing has been practised for thousands of years, tribal rituals and challenges preceded it. These rituals often involved initiation ceremonies where participants had to attain certain levels of performance in order to achieve acceptance in their tribe. It is important to be accepted and recognized by others but it is even more important to accept your talents and to recognize your achievements.

6. FLYING

Dream

Flying dreams often begin with the sensation of floating. As you realize that the force of gravity is no longer weighing you down, you soar into the sky and begin to fly through the air. You seem to steer by just imagining the direction you want to go in and you have a tremendous feeling of exhilaration. Sometimes you may be flying on your own, like a superhero, and at other times you may be in an aircraft or unusual vehicle. In some flying dreams you may feel like a passenger but you feel most liberated when you are controlling your flight path.

Meaning

When you dream of flying, you feel as if you are being released from some limitation or obligation in your waking life. Much of our language around our obligations involves metaphors that are based on weight. We speak of the *'gravity of the situation'* or *'a weighty decision'* and when we are released from a heavy responsibility we often describe it as *'walking on air'*. The flying dream reflects this sense of liberation and shows you have been released from circumstances that were weighing you down in some way. The removal of this burden frees you up to make your choices and act on them without any constraints, giving you the feeling of flying *'free as a bird'*, swooping and soaring without limitation.

This freedom of choice often occurs during the creative process when you are expressing your unique talents as you transcend mere practicalities and procedures, raising your game far beyond them. If you find it difficult to get off the ground or encounter obstacles in your flying dreams, it usually suggests there is a situation that you are still too attached to in your daily life. When you find yourself flying an unusual vehicle, this shows you have a unique skill that gives you a great sense of liberation when you use it. Being a passenger indicates you are currently in a situation that gives you some freedom but not as much as if you were in charge of taking your own direction.

Action

This dream reflects how you are releasing yourself from limitations in your waking life and feeling more liberated than

usual. Although you may regard this feeling of liberation as just luck or coincidence, it is usually because you have managed to create an opportunity for yourself. It can be worthwhile to consider other opportunities and chances in your daily life where you can take yourself off into the realms of new possibilities. To sustain your flying dreams, try to avoid airy-fairy thinking and ensure you have a solid platform for launching your ideas and a safe and appropriate place to land them.

Background

Although we have only been able to experience powered flight since the early 20th century, the sky has been linked to the powers of our imaginations for tens of thousands of years. We can't see the top of our heads without a mirror and this can often give the feeling that our heads and our soaring imaginings are open to the wide blue yonder above. The sky has come to represent how the human imagination is one of the most powerful gifts we possess. In most religions and mythical cultures, the most powerful deity is the one who rules the sky.

7. FALLING

Dream

The sensation of falling in a dream often seems to happen without any warning. Everything seems normal and under control but then you suddenly feel your legs give way as you stumble and fall. Sometimes the fall may seem to be a small one as you trip over a kerb or lurch into a pothole. At other times, the plunge might be more dramatic as you tumble down endless stairs or plummet down a cliff into a deep chasm. There seems to be nothing you can do to prevent your fall and you may feel yourself suddenly stop as you hit the ground.

Meaning

Falling dreams are often associated with some form of perceived failure in waking life. They are usually triggered by the sudden realization that you will not be able to completely control the outcome of a particular situation. You have probably set yourself high standards for the results you expect and you may feel like a failure if you aren't able to reach them. This can bring you down to earth with a bump and make you feel like you are letting others down as well as yourself. Sometimes, however, you need to release yourself from your responsibilities and the sensation of falling in dreams comes from this inevitable process of letting go. As you let go, you give yourself the freedom to move on.

When you fall asleep, you are releasing yourself from conscious awareness so that you can relax and repair your body, and give yourself the opportunity to dream. When you dream of falling, it is usually because your body is relaxing and you are releasing accumulated tension from your muscles. If you trip over a small obstacle, such as a kerb, it often indicates that you are just releasing some minor tension from your daily life. A larger fall suggests you need to let go of some bigger responsibilities that are dragging you down. Hitting the ground indicates you need to take a more down-to-earth approach, getting your feet firmly back on the ground as you work out a way forward.

Action

This dream is often triggered by accumulated stress and tension, and so is encouraging you to take a more relaxed approach in certain areas of your waking life. Most of your residual muscle tension can be released by physically relaxing before going to bed. Muscular tension often arises from a fear of failure and it can feel like you spend most of your day braced for impact. When you are tense you are far less likely to notice opportunities and take full advantage of them. The more you relax, the more you can influence favourable outcomes.

Background

The phrase we use to describe entering our sleeping state is *'falling asleep'* and so we tend to associate relaxing with falling and letting go. As our large anti-gravity muscles, such as our back and legs and arms, relax we physically sink a little lower into our bed. This release of tension is often experienced as a muscle twitch known as the hypnic jerk. If we are on the edge of sleep or have fallen asleep, then we usually feel that we are actually falling. Falling is often associated with failure in our language, such as *'being let go'* or *'falling from grace'*.

8. OUT OF CONTROL VEHICLE

Dream

You are travelling in a vehicle that seems to have gone out of control. The vehicle is most often a car but may be any form of motorized transport. No matter how carefully you try

to proceed, the vehicle never goes where you want and it often spins uncontrollably and dangerously. You desperately try to slow down and come to a halt because you are scared about crashing into things and damaging the car, or hurting yourself and your passengers. You may also find yourself going backwards down a hill as you frantically try to use the brakes but they have little or no effect.

Meaning

Dreaming about a vehicle indicates you are thinking about the path that you are currently taking through life. This is often a career path and you are usually considering how you can further yourself professionally. The most common vehicle in the dream is a car because this symbolizes your personal drive and ambition. Larger mass transport vehicles, such as trains or buses, tend to represent teams or organizations you may be a part of. Although you may have a plan that you are carefully trying to put into practice, you aren't able to follow the direction in which you really want to go. Circumstances seem to be getting out of hand and the more you try to control the situation, the more disconnected you seem to become from it.

An imminent crash shows you are going to be in contact or conflict with something unavoidable. If you find yourself going backwards in the vehicle, particularly downhill, it shows you may be trying to reverse a decision or back out of a commitment. Loss of brakes shows that some conflict with others may be inevitable. You would like to manoeuvre out of the circumstances that you have found yourself in, but are concerned that it might be difficult to extricate yourself. Although you may feel withdrawing is the best way to resolve this tension, the only way forward is to regain control by facing up to the challenge that lies in front of you.

Action

Rather than abandoning your present position, try considering the areas where you do have control. Some of these areas might not be obvious and may also require you to influence someone instead of trying to specifically control their behaviour. Don't be afraid to ask for help from others as they can help you take charge of the situation and put you firmly back in the driver's seat. It may be difficult to accept that there are some situations that you really have no control over, but the more you try to control uncertainty, the more out of control you usually feel.

Background

When learning to control any sort of vehicle, there are often situations where the task seems completely overwhelming. If the vehicle does not seem to be responding to our attempts to manoeuvre it, it may seem as if it has a mind of its own. Personal transport is often associated with where we plan to go in life and what we want to achieve, and we hear this in phrases like *'a vehicle for my ambitions'* and *'the road to success'*. We also describe our motivations as our *'drives'*, and how *'driven'* certain people are as they progress towards a particular goal.

9. FINDING AN UNUSED ROOM

Dream

You are walking through your house when you notice a door that you are sure you haven't seen before. Even though you may have lived in the place for years, you can't remember opening the door during that time. The door seems strangely familiar, however, and you open it with a mixture of trepidation and excitement. You are surprised to find a room that you had completely forgotten about. Sometimes the position of the room in your house may seem to be architecturally impossible and it may be that the door opens on to a whole series of rooms or part of a much larger building.

Meaning

When you dream about your house, it often represents your self and the different rooms symbolize different aspects of your character. The doors to the rooms reflect how you express and access these different parts of yourself. Discovering a previously unnoticed door in a dream usually indicates that you have the opportunity to step into an exciting new possibility in your waking life. The room the door opens into is often familiar because it represents a talent that you were passionate about in the past but had to step away from for a while. For some reason you had to close the door on this opportunity and forget about it but now you have the chance to step back into the potential that it holds.

This dream often occurs when some space opens up in your waking life and you have the time to return to your old passion. The size of the room reflects the magnitude of the opportunity and the room often seems to stretch off into the distance, or leads on to a whole series of other rooms. This indicates that exploring the initial possibility will lead onto a number of other exciting opportunities and give you the chance to expand well beyond where you are just now. The contents of the room reflect the nature of the talent or passion that you closed the door on. They may be a bit dusty or rusty but they are still intact and waiting for you to put them back into regular use.

Action

Even though you think you know your achievements and your limitations, you have unknown talents you have yet to discover. The chance to explore this talent often comes in the form of an unexpected opportunity. Like any room it can take some time to realize the best way to use it as you furnish your ambition. You need to be open to opportunity and not close the door on any chances that you create. As you begin to explore one talent, you often start to become aware of other possibilities for using your unique abilities.

Background

One of the main ways we learn is by making analogies, and one of the first analogies we make is using our house to symbolize our own self. A house has an inside and an outside and we all have an inner life and an outer life. Space is usually at a premium in most of our houses and the number of rooms it contains most often reflects its value. In the same way that houses can be extended to provide more room, the more that we extend our abilities, the more often we encounter valuable character-building opportunities.

10. BEING LATE

Dream

You thought you had plenty of time to reach your appointment but you have just realized how late it is getting. You rush to get ready, looking at the clock, unable to understand how so much time has passed. As you try to reach your rendezvous, you keep being frustrated by obstacles and distractions. You become involved in dealing with these frustrations and are dismayed to find they eat up even more of your precious time. It starts to feel as if your time isn't your own and that you will never reach where you want to be.

Meaning

When you dream of being late, you are starting to feel that you are about to lose the opportunity to experience some sort of fulfilment in your waking life. The appointment or deadline in the dream is often a timetable that you have set in day-to-day life to achieve a specific ambition, such as starting a family or reaching a professional qualification. You realize that time is running out if you want to accomplish this goal. Looking at the clock shows you have been filling your life with lots of other activities but are beginning to realize it isn't getting you anywhere. Even though you may think that you have been working towards fulfilling your objective, you have just been going through the motions.

The more you rush to meet your appointment with your objective, then the more the opportunity seems to disappear. You may try different routes to your goal but none of them take you where you want and it is leaving you feeling frustrated and distracted. This suggests you have been avoiding certain decisions that will commit you to a particular course of action in waking life. The more you procrastinate about this decision, the more of your time that you use up. When you actually make the commitment to purposeful action, however, then you start taking responsibility for the outcome. The more committed your action, the more time you will make to ensure your success, rather than constantly looking at the clock.

Action

The timely message from this dream is about committing to meaningful action rather than just involving yourself in busy and meaningless activity. Until you commit to a decision, you will always find yourself hesitating and using your time ineffectively. As soon as you commit yourself to definite action, you will find a range of opportunities opening up that will help you fulfil your goals. Once your decision is made, your direction becomes clear and you can plan your progress according to your timetable. Your time becomes your own, rather than being subject to the whims and vagaries of what is happening around you.

Background

Although we think of the measurement of time using calendars and clocks as a relatively recent advance, we have based our lives on certain rhythms since prehistoric times. Using the cycles of the sun and the moon, we observed the progression of natural events and then used them to choose the most opportune times to take action. In our hectic modern world, time has become our most precious commodity and there never seems to be enough of it. The more purposeful we are in our actions, however, the more we can make time for what really counts.

11. SEARCHING FOR SOMETHING

Dream

In this dream, you are constantly searching for something but you aren't sure exactly what you are looking for. You may be

hunting through your home, looking in different rooms and cupboards, or perhaps out in your garden or the street outside. Your search may take place in an office or a factory or you might be driving around looking for something. As the search takes you further afield, you may use trains to go to distant towns or an aeroplane to fly to foreign countries. No matter how much you search, you never seem to find what you are looking for.

Meaning

When you find yourself searching for something in a dream, you are often trying to discover a sense of deeper fulfilment in your waking life. Not knowing what you are searching for reflects the fact that you aren't consciously aware of what will make you feel more fulfilled in your daily existence. If the search is taking place in your home then you are trying to find some hidden aspects of your character that will make you feel more complete. Although you know that you have potential talents locked away inside, you are searching for ways to connect with them. With every door you open and every cupboard you look in, you hope to discover the part of yourself that you are looking for.

If you are searching outside in your garden or in the street, you are looking for a greater feeling of fulfilment and recognition within your social circle. Looking for something in an office or a factory indicates that you would like to be more accomplished professionally. If you are driving along a road, or at a station or airport, you are searching to see how you can achieve greater satisfaction in your career. In all these situations, what you are really looking for is your true purpose in life. Rather than constantly searching outside, your real sense of purpose can be found most easily by searching inside yourself. Exploring your fundamental needs and motivations will always help you find a deeper purpose.

Action

The message from this dream is that you are trying to find what would make you feel happiest and most fulfilled in your life. You aren't sure, however, what would give you the most satisfaction, so you spend most of your time hoping you might just stumble across it by chance. Rather than running around and constantly searching, it is easier just to stand still because the answer to what you are looking for is already inside you. Ask yourself what you want most out of life and then quietly wait for the answer to appear.

Background

Human beings are great opportunists and one of the reasons for our success is our willingness to explore the unknown and search out valuable resources. Although our modern needs may have become more complex since our time as hunter-gatherers, we are always searching for something of value and the ability to express our values and talents. Some of the first games we learn to play as children involve searching for something, such as peek-a-boo and hide-and-seek, where we purposely hide so that we can search and have the joy of finding each other.

12. CLIMBING UP A HILL

Dream

You are on your way to somewhere important and have to ascend a steep hill in order to reach your destination. As you

progress, you often find that the gradient gets steeper and the going gets rougher. Your route often narrows to a track or a stony path and you may end up trying to climb a steep cliff. As you cling onto this sheer rock face and try to make progress, you might find the rock becoming loose and starting to crumble around you. You may also find yourself climbing up an ever-steepening staircase.

Meaning

Dreaming of climbing uphill indicates that you are making a sustained effort to obtain a particular level of achievement in your waking life. Like ascending an incline, trying to achieve a higher level of success often requires a greater commitment of energy and determination. The gradient often becomes steeper in the dream because you may have underestimated the effort and resources required to reach your objective. The steeper the ascent, then the steeper the learning curve you have to negotiate as you progress towards your goal. The going underfoot may become rougher as you find it more challenging to gain traction and maintain momentum in waking life. The path may peter out as your ascent takes you off the beaten track and into unknown territory.

Your way forward often becomes a sheer rock face as you come to terms with the hard realities and sheer effort involved in making further progress. Clinging onto the cliff face shows that you are trying to keep a tight grip on your situation but are concerned things might get out of hand. The rock crumbling around you indicates you feel that some of your previously solid support is crumbling and this is making you feel desperately insecure. Climbing a staircase shows that you are thinking about a particular career path and your steady upward progression.

A spiral staircase suggests that, even though you are making continued upward progress, it often feels like you are just going round in circles.

Action

The message from this dream is that you will achieve your ambitions but it will probably require a steady plod at a measured pace rather than a short-term all-out effort. Rather than rushing at the tasks ahead of you, it may be better to slow your pace and change down a gear so you can keep moving, no matter how steep the challenge ahead of you seems. You may have to take it one step at a time and if you are feeling insecure, don't be afraid to ask for help from someone to guide you to safer and higher ground.

Background

We often describe our potential to succeed in terms of height and so we speak about being a *'high achiever'* or having *'lofty ambitions'*. From the first time we ascend a staircase, however, we know that climbing uphill takes more effort than walking along the flat. This leads to our vocabulary containing phrases such as *'an uphill struggle'* or *'having a mountain to climb'*. We also describe reaching higher levels of achievement as *'raising our game'* and *'gaining the higher ground'*. As you ramp up your efforts, however, it often gives you a much better perspective on the new horizons that are opening up for you.

13. UNEXPECTEDLY FALLING IN LOVE

Dream

Much to your amazement, you find yourself becoming involved in an unusual romance or unexpectedly falling in love. This love affair often comes as a complete surprise as you realize that you are being drawn towards someone who you don't usually find attractive in any way. It may be a work colleague or someone who doesn't conform to your usual gender preferences. You may be even more intrigued as you realize that you are falling in love with an inanimate item. Every time you see the object of your affections, your heart leaps and you may feel slightly guilty.

Meaning

When you dream of unexpectedly falling in love, there is some very valuable part of your character that you have suddenly started to become more aware of. The dream usually comes as a complete surprise and you may find it very unsettling, particularly your choice of romantic partner. Although you normally wouldn't be attracted towards this person, they embody a character trait that you find very desirable, though usually not in a romantic way. You are beginning to realize that you also have the potential to demonstrate this personal quality and you find this possibility to be very exciting. The strength of your attraction may seem quite out of character, however, puzzling you as to why you are being drawn to this particular trait.

If the object of your affections is decisive and ambitious, then you are becoming more aware of your power to make choices and starting to have a clearer idea of what you really want to accomplish in your life. Someone outside your gender preferences indicates that you are becoming much more comfortable with your own femininity or masculinity. Falling in love with an object suggests that you are bringing to life whatever qualities you associate with that item. All these possible situations reflect that you are actually falling in love with your purpose and potential. This blossoming romance with yourself isn't some vain and narcissistic affair but an increasing acceptance of your abilities and attractiveness.

Action

The message from this dream is that you are unexpectedly becoming far more aware of your potential and are feeling much more confident about yourself. This new level of awareness, however, can be quite confusing at first and may cause some disruption in your daily routine. It can be tempting to shy away from exploring your recently revealed potential but it holds vital information. By opening up to the possibility that there might be much more to your talents than you previously thought, you can begin to attract what you need and who you desire into your life.

Background

Like our dreams, we usually think of love as something that happens to us, rather than something we create. True love seems so precious and valuable that our culture surrounds us with stories of unexpected romance. In books, films, plays, poems and songs, it sometimes seems as if all human stories are love stories. This constant searching for true love reflects

that one of our most fundamental needs as social animals is to love and be loved. The phrase *'falling in love'* reflects the more we relax and let go, the more fully we can accept our selves and our unique gifts.

14. HAUNTED BY GHOSTS

Dream

You keep seeing a shadowy figure out of the corner of your eye and, although the person seems vaguely familiar, you can't quite place them. As you look more closely at them, you realize they are partially transparent, and are shocked to realize he or she is a ghost. You try to escape from them but they keep following you and no matter what you do, you just can't shake them off. They seem to be everywhere you look and every time you hear a strange noise or see an odd reflection, you are sure it must be them.

Meaning

When you dream about being haunted by a ghost, there is some aspect of your past that you are trying to lay to rest in your waking life. Even though the ghost may not resemble you, it reflects some aspect of yourself that you thought was dead and buried. This aspect is a habit or a memory from your past, which is coming back to haunt you in some way. You may be trying to ignore this memory in your waking life because you think there is no substance to it and so the ghost appears transparent and insubstantial. No matter how much you try to escape and hide, the ghost is always there because it is part of you and your life so far.

These habits and memories usually appear in your waking life as particular behavioural patterns and the more you try to ignore these hauntingly familiar behaviours, the more the ghost will draw your attention to them. Such behaviours can often frustrate you and absorb an enormous amount of your time and effort. By confronting your habitual patterns and starting to resolve them, however, you may often release a lot of creative energy. Your creativity can help to breathe new life into your ideas or resurrect a valuable gift or talent from your past. This talent is a unique quality and intrinsic to you and no matter how much you try ignoring it, it will always be part of you.

Action

This dream is drawing your attention to the fact that there is some experience from your past that you have dismissed as being of no substance. This event, however, is actually continuing to have a substantial effect in your current life and you really need to lay it to rest. This past experience has locked up a potentially valuable part of your character and it is time to confront it rather than always allowing yourself to be spooked by it. Instead of being possessed by your past, it is time to claim back your talent and own it yourself.

Background

As our ancestors explored the mystery of death, ghosts became a way of explaining the inexplicable and the insubstantial. Ghostly apparitions are believed to be the spirits of the dead and have come to symbolize parts of us that aren't physically manifested. Although we attempt to rationalize strange occurrences in our contemporary culture, we continue to be drawn to the mysteries of ghosts and the spirit world. Many people use the latest technology in their efforts to confirm the presence of ghosts and some of our favourite stories feature ghostly characters and haunted houses.

15. RETURN OF AN EX-LOVER

Dream

You are surprised to find yourself making love with an ex-lover. Even though you can't imagine how you got yourself into this situation and feel really guilty about it, you are also very excited. You try to discuss the situation rationally with your lover in the dream but keep getting distracted by the passionate intensity of your feelings and end up making love with them again and again. No matter how you try and leave their loving embrace, you are really enjoying being so intimate with them. You eventually manage to get away but have lingering feelings of unrequited love.

Meaning

When you dream of making love with an ex-lover, some situation in your current waking life is triggering an awareness of the qualities that you most powerfully associate with them. Rather than being a wish-fulfilment that you want to get back with your lover, you are using your ex to symbolize a growing awareness of these characteristics within yourself. Making love with that person suggests that you are becoming far more

intimately aware of these qualities in your character. If your ex was unreliable and untruthful, then you are letting yourself down in some way by not facing up to the truth. A warm and generous ex shows that you are discovering your warmth and generosity and are being encouraged to express it.

An ex often appears in a dream to warn you not to repeat past relationship patterns with a current romantic partner and this is an encouragement to let go of old behaviours that no longer serve you. You may have been too accommodating with your ex and you may be playing out this pattern again in your current relationship. Sexual dreams can also be experienced when you are becoming particularly excited about a new creative idea or project. Dreaming of the procreative act reflects that you possess the spark to create something new and unique, and then bring it to life. No matter how much you try to ignore this idea, you are urging yourself to embrace this exciting prospect.

Action

This dream is arousing you to connect with a higher level of your self-awareness. The more aware that you are about yourself, the more you will understand your needs, particularly if you are involved in an intimate relationship. As this dream illuminates your fundamental identity and needs, it also helps to reveal the deeper sexual and romantic truths of what you really need within a loving relationship. By being more aware of what qualities you are attracted to in a lover, you can make conscious decisions about how to attract the intimate partner of your dreams.

Background

Although we often think that an intimate relationship is all about our encounters with another person, one of the main

revelations we experience is an increased awareness of ourselves. The more we open up to another person and disclose our vulnerabilities, the more intensely aware we become of ourselves. New relationships and love affairs are usually when we encounter the most intense episodes of self-discovery and so when we discover anything new about ourselves, whether in a relationship or not, we tend to equate these deep and passionate feelings with it.

16. AIRCRAFT CRASH

Dream

A big jet airliner is plummeting from the sky and you just know that there is going to be a terrible crash. The aircraft seems to level out just above the ground, however, and continues flying at a really low altitude, just scraping between buildings or trees. It may crash-land and break into pieces, and you are surprised to see passengers walking out unharmed from the wreckage. You might be watching this from the ground or may actually be onboard the aircraft itself. If you are onboard, you might try and take control of the aircraft to guide it into land.

Meaning

When you dream about an aircraft crash, you have some concerns about a plan or project you are involved with in waking life. The sky symbolizes your thinking space and aeroplanes represent how your plans can be steered towards successful

conclusions. The bigger the aeroplane, the more ambitious the plan, so dreaming about an airliner usually represents a large project involving a number of people. Although the project has been well planned and seems to be valid in theory, your confidence in it is plummeting and you are concerned that it is going to come down to earth with a bang. But just when it seems like the project will end in an unsatisfactory conclusion, it is able to continue but at a lower level than before.

Scraping along between trees and buildings shows that the people involved in the project are finding it difficult to make their plans really take off and are having to deal with a variety of obstacles in their path. If the aeroplane does make contact with the ground and breaks up, it usually indicates the project is being terminated and may be split up into smaller and more manageable pieces. Passengers walking unharmed from the wreckage show that those involved in the project are free to move on to other opportunities. If you are onboard the aircraft, it shows that you are actively involved in this project rather than viewing from the outside. Taking control shows that you have the ability to guide it towards a successful outcome.

Action

The message from this dream is to consider the current trajectory of a project or a plan in which you are involved. Although the concern for most projects is getting them off the ground, any pilot will tell you take-off is the easy part. The hard part is landing the project and ensuring the safe and secure passage of everyone involved in it. Rather than being involved in some flight of fancy, plan the project in as much detail as you can. It is also valuable to have a contingency plan, in case you are diverted by some unforeseen event.

Background

Although aeroplanes are a recent invention in human history, our ancestors used to dream of being borne aloft on the wings of eagles. These dreams evolved into myths such as that of Daedalus and Icarus who made wings so they could transport themselves through the sky. In many of these myths, the wings fail and the flier plummets to the ground as airy theory is confronted by hard reality. We now take air travel almost for granted and it has become commonplace to use phrases such as *'let's get this thing off the ground'* and *'in a holding pattern'* to describe our plans and projects.

17. CHILDREN IN JEOPARDY

Dream

You are shocked to realize that your children are in some sort of jeopardy and feel as if you have let them down by allowing this situation to occur. It may be that your children are facing terrible danger or about to be involved in a horrible accident. You might have forgotten where you left them and are trying desperately to find them before it's too late. Even though you thought they were in a safe place, you are sure that they must now be in mortal peril. You can't believe you were so foolish as to leave them on their own.

Meaning

When you dream about a child, you are usually thinking about some situation or cause that is very close to your heart in

waking life. It can be easy to think this dream is a premonition and your child is in actual danger. You are using your child, however, as a symbol to represent an idea that is very precious to you and that you are trying to nurture and develop in some way. If there are a number of children in your dream, then these represent a number of growth possibilities that you are closely involved in at the moment. Although you may be giving these opportunities lots of encouragement and attention, you feel their continued existence is in some sort of jeopardy.

Your ambitions appear to be in danger of being unrealized because you think that you don't currently have the time or energy that they really need to have devoted to them. You feel there is a danger that your projects might come to an untimely end or that they might be accidentally cancelled because no one else realizes how important they are to you. Although you are desperate to reconnect with your ambitions, you are finding it difficult to pick them up where you left off and now your plans may seem in quite a precarious state. By realizing that your ambitions are under threat, however, you can use your resilience and resourcefulness to bring them back to life.

Action

This dream is actively drawing your attention to a precious personal gift that you have been neglecting. You may have been hoping that your idea would just grow and develop without much input from you but, in reality, it demands far more care and attention than you have been able to provide so far. This level of nurturing is required until the project is more independent and can survive without your full-time support. This precious gift is also usually an embodiment of your inner child, and reflects your potential to create something new and exciting.

Background

Finding an unprotected and vulnerable child is one of the most emotive situations that we can experience. Our immediate instinct is to rescue any child in distress, even though it involves jeopardizing our own safety and security. A child's cry of alarm will cut through any other noises and we will immediately give their welfare top priority, especially if it is one of our children. If our children seem content and secure, however, it can also be easy to lose sight of them in our immediate awareness, leaving them up to their own devices as they play and explore.

18. PUBLIC PERFORMANCE

Dream

You have been given the opportunity to perform in public in front of a live audience but nothing seems to be working. There seems to be something wrong with the sound equipment and you have to keep unplugging cables and reconnecting them to try and make yourself heard. As you start your performance, you might forget your lines or find that your words come out all jumbled up or in the wrong order. The audience begin to get restless and you feel really frustrated because you know you can perform this piece perfectly but events seem to be conspiring against you.

Meaning

Dreaming of performing in public reflects your need to have your abilities recognized and appreciated by a wider

audience. These abilities may be creative talents or they might be professional skills you employ in your job. Although you undoubtedly possess these talents and skills, you are finding it difficult to have them acknowledged by other people. It may be easy to blame the conditions that you are trying to perform under but your lack of recognition is usually because you find it difficult to accept praise from others in your daily life. This can make you seem aloof and unconcerned about other people's opinions, even though you are desperate to be recognized and accepted by them.

Your aloofness can lead to a feeling of disconnection from your friends and colleagues and you often try to compensate for this by tinkering around with technicalities, trying to hide behind the technology you use. Your lack of connection also results in you becoming disconnected from your true feelings and the ability to say what you really want to say. Instead of speaking from your heart with your authentic voice, you may try to communicate in a distant manner. This can result in you forgetting who you really are and becoming confused about what you really want to say and do. The most important audience member is always yourself and this dream shows that you are becoming frustrated and restless with your perceived lack of recognition.

Action

The insight from this dream is that performances are about being able to accept your talent as much as displaying it. It can be easy to hope that you will be accepted and recognized by other people but it is far more challenging to do this if you find it difficult to recognize and accept your talent. The more praise you give to others, the more likely you will be able to accept and relish your skills. The more confident you are and the more generous you are with your praise, the more relaxed you will be about performing with your unique abilities.

Background

We are encouraged to perform from an early age, whether it is for a family party piece or a school play. Much of our success and recognition from others is often about saying the right thing at the right time and performing the appropriate actions. Many of our favourite TV shows are based on the judging of talents in a public performance and we spend a lot of our time looking for the approval of others rather than just accepting ourselves. The more accepting we are of our gifts, then the more spontaneously and easier we find it to share and perform them.

19. TIDAL WAVE

Dream

You are standing at the edge of the sea on a beach or a shoreline when you see a massive wall of water hurtling towards you. You may have time to run away up a hill but often you can't escape from the onrushing tidal wave because it is moving so quickly. As the water engulfs you, you find yourself rolling and tumbling, and completely disoriented. Somehow you manage to swim free and end up on the beach, gasping for breath and looking at the wave as it recedes into the distance. Sometimes the wave does not actually break but just hovers above you, a short distance from the shore.

Meaning

When you dream about water, you are reflecting on your feelings and emotions, and how they flow through you. Like your feelings, water often appears to be fluid and unpredictable and a tidal wave represents an apparently overwhelming surge of emotion that is sweeping through your waking life. Earthquakes often trigger tidal waves and this huge emotional surge may have been triggered by a seismic shift in one of your major relationships. This significant change is flooding through all parts of your life and is threatening to engulf you. Your initial reaction is often to make an effort to raise yourself above all the emotional uproar. By claiming the moral higher ground, you hope to view the situation with some detachment.

You may, however, become engulfed in wave after wave of seemingly uncontrollable emotions. This can completely disorient you, making your heart sink and your head spin. Although you sometimes feel like the situation is really dragging you down, you manage to navigate your way through the chaos to a feeling of stability. Even though you might be feeling all washed-up and crestfallen, you know this emotional turbulence, like all waves, will recede and fade into the distance. If the wave is hovering just offshore as you stand on the shore, this suggests that you are aware of a potential emotional disruption but you are taking a more objective view of your feelings, standing your ground until the turmoil passes.

Action

This dream is reflecting your concerns about being engulfed by your emotions as you try and navigate your way through a period of major change. The situation is probably out of your

control, so instead of trying to contain it, you may just have to accept it. Rather than fully immersing yourself in the emotional chaos, try standing back and giving yourself a more objective view of your current circumstances. Although you may be trying to resist this change, you know deep down that it is inevitable.

Background

Much of our language about our emotions is water-based, such as a *'surge of elation'*, *'ebbing enthusiasm'*, or *'an outpouring of grief'*. Like our feelings, water seems to have its own rhythms and flows. Through experience, we also come to realize that, like water, our feelings can be incredibly powerful and can have deep and far-reaching effects on the rest of our lives. The more aware that we become of our moods and rhythms, the more we realize that we can't really contain our emotions, we can only ever hope to guide and influence them.

20. ENCOUNTERING A DEAD LOVED ONE

Dream

You are surprised and delighted to encounter a loved one, even though you were absolutely certain that they had passed away in real life. Here they are as large as life, however, and speaking with you as if they were still alive. The loved one is someone who you had a very close connection with and often tends to

be a close relative, such as a parent or grandparent. They may try to give you a message and although they are usually really pleased to see you, they may sometimes seem to be really angry with you.

Meaning

Dreaming of an encounter with a dead relative or loved one suggests that you are undergoing a transformation in your personal awareness in daily life. Although your loved one has passed away in waking life, you recreate them in your dreams using your memories of them and your experiences of their personal qualities. Your encounter with them usually indicates that you are becoming more aware of these characteristic qualities starting to appear in your behaviour patterns. If your father loved you with a wise and mature authority when he was alive, then his appearance suggests that you are becoming more comfortable with your wisdom and authority. If your grandmother was nurturing and affectionate, then an encounter with her shows your increasing capacity for loving and caring.

If your loved one is trying to give you a message, then you are usually trying to communicate something to yourself in waking life. The nature of the message shows what you are trying to tell yourself and it often involves the discovery of a personal resource or talent you were unaware that you possessed. Although you may have had an excellent relationship with your loved one in waking life, it may surprise you to find them being angry and upset with you in your dream. Rather than them actually being angry with you, however, this shows that you are angry with your loved one for passing on and leaving you apparently abandoned and without them.

Action

This dream is reconnecting you with a part of yourself that you thought you had lost forever. It can often seem like your loved one has actually visited you in this dream but you are actually being reunited with what they really meant to you. One of the gifts your loved one gave you was the ability to see qualities in you that you often could not see yourself. Rather than always being resigned to just mourning their passing, it is time to embrace and embody all the qualities that your loved one illuminated for you.

Background

Losing a loved one is one of the saddest and most painful experiences we have to endure. It often seems as if our loved one contained part of us and we have lost that part of our identity forever. Even though they may no longer be here in this physical existence with us, however, they can still continue to connect us with the qualities that made us so special to them. Although losing a loved one is heart-achingly sad, we can continue to look to them for a much deeper love and inspiration.

21. HAVING AN AFFAIR

Dream

You are almost certain that your romantic partner is having an affair. They are coming home late, seem distracted and appear to have lost all interest in you. Although you frantically

search for clues, you can't find anything that definitely proves their infidelity. Your suspicions are confirmed, however, when you find some pictures of them with another lover, or walk into a room and find them clinched in a passionate embrace with another person. Even though you are devastated at your discovery, you are satisfied that your fears were justified. No matter how angry you are, you still feel terribly let down by your lover.

Meaning

Dreaming that your partner is being unfaithful is usually triggered when you begin to lose faith in your own sexiness and attractiveness in waking life. Although it can be tempting to think that your partner has been spending intimate time with someone far more alluring, this dream often reflects that you are losing touch with some of your fundamental needs, making you feel less attractive than usual. This can often happen when a situation in your daily life is frustrating you and causing you to lose confidence in yourself. Your frustration and lack of self-assurance usually occur, however, when you stop trusting your judgement and start looking to others for their approval and appreciation.

Your need for approval can lead you to abandoning ambitions that are close to your heart, and although you might rationalize that you are doing it in your best interests, you unconsciously feel that you have let yourself down. This can make you feel bored and impatient with yourself and, instead of voicing your feelings in waking life, you project your unresolved restlessness onto your significant other. Rather than sharing your frustrations with your current partner, you may even start hoping that some other potential lover will find you attractive and you might end up daydreaming about having an affair yourself. The more confident that you are in waking life, the more confidently you can step into your new future and become the person you always dream of being.

Action

This dream is letting you know you that you are betraying yourself in some way. You are losing faith in your abilities and are probably relying too much on approval from other people to make you feel needed and special. Rather than constantly looking to others to make you feel attractive and bolster your confidence, this dream is encouraging you to just be yourself. It can be easy to allow others to have the responsibility for your hopes and aspirations but it is now time for you to reaffirm your faith in your purpose and potential.

Background

In our intimate relationships, we tend to project our feelings of self-worth and self-esteem on to our intimate partners. This is particularly true in new relationships where we often view our new partner as a prize who reflects our deepest desires, rather than an ever-present and supportive pillar. We can end up feeling that our partner is somehow responsible for our happiness and fulfilment and, when we are unhappy with ourselves, it can be far too easy to place the responsibility on them instead of having more faith in our abilities.

22. ENDLESS PACKING

Dream

You are trying to pack your bags as you prepare for an important trip and you know that you have to leave very soon. There always seem to be more bags to be packed and you are concerned that you don't have enough room to take all the things you need for your journey. Even when you think you have managed to cram everything into your luggage, you find even more possessions that have to be stowed away somewhere. You realize that you will never manage to finish your packing if you want to leave in time to start your trip.

Meaning

When you dream of endless packing, you are thinking about how you constantly try to organize your waking life so you can pack as much as possible into it. Although you always attempt to cram as much as you can into your day, it seems as if there is never enough time and there is always too much to be done. Your luggage symbolizes your potential for fulfilment and your resourcefulness in carrying out all your plans and ambitions. The feeling of having to leave soon suggests that you would like to fulfil these particular ambitions by a specific deadline. But no matter how busily you try to organize yourself, you always feel as if there is still something missing from your life.

Even though you seem to be frantically cramming as much as you can into your life, you feel constantly frustrated because it appears as if you are going nowhere. Most of the work you do in your waking life is about preparing for success rather than actually committing to a particular course of action where you may have to step into the unknown to achieve your goals. All the items you are packing into your bags represent experiences and habits from your past but your need to be prepared for every eventuality is actually holding you back. Even though these resources might prove to be of some use in exploring your new direction, you can end up feeling weighed down by your expectations.

Action

This dream is showing you how you can make the most of a new opportunity by letting go of some old baggage from the past. It can be easy to burden yourself with assumptions about what you might need to make the most of this chance. The best way to achieve success, however, is usually to spend less time preparing and more time actually working towards your goal. The more that you prepare, the more likely that you will fall into old patterns of behaviour as you try and control the outcome of this new situation.

Background

Ever since humans began using tools, leading a nomadic hunting and gathering existence, we have used bags to hold and transport our possessions. At first these were small bags, which perhaps contained valuable resources such as a few flints or some herbs, and helped prepare us for any unknown eventuality. As our lives have become richer and more complex, however, so has the volume of baggage we encumber ourselves with. The word *'encumber'* is derived from the Old French word *combre*, meaning *'a dam'*, and the more we weigh ourselves down with expectations, the less freely our lives seem to flow.

23. GUILTY OF A CRIME

Dream

For some reason, you have committed a terrible crime and are desperately trying to cover it up. Sometimes the offence can seem particularly serious like murder and you are trying to dispose of the body. No matter how hard you try to conceal the evidence, there is always a clue left behind such as a foot or a hand sticking out or a phone message that you can't erase. You try to escape but are terrified that someone will discover your misdeed. The crime often seems like an accident or something you were forced to do in order to protect yourself.

Meaning

When you dream of being guilty of a crime, you are feeling responsible for letting yourself down in some way in your waking life. Although you always try to do the right thing and have certain principles that you live your life by, you feel that you have betrayed your moral code. Dreaming that you have committed a murder and are disposing of the body usually indicates that you are trying to eliminate some aspect of your character. This aspect is often a unique talent or a creative skill that you feel you are being forced to give up because of your current circumstances. Even though you would like to continue with it, you are sacrificing it to make other people happy.

Although you may try to conceal all evidence of your hidden talent in waking life, it keeps bursting out and you can't help but draw attention to it. Dreaming that you have stolen something valuable indicates that you aren't valuing yourself enough. Stealing symbolizes taking something without permission and it may feel as if you aren't giving yourself permission to enjoy yourself spontaneously without any deeper responsibilities. Your desire to escape reflects your need to escape your self-limiting beliefs and give yourself the freedom to be who you really want to be in your life. The crime often seems like an accident or self-protection because you are trying to ensure that others will accept you.

Action

The evidence from this dream is that you are trying to cover up some of your deepest needs in order to meet the wishes of other people and so gain their approval. Allowing other people to judge you, however, can often result in you losing the freedom to truly express yourself. Trying to conform to the wishes of others to gain their love and acceptance can often result in you being disloyal to your fundamental needs. By giving yourself permission to behave more naturally, you can set yourself free from the demands of others and liberate your genuine talents.

Background

Even before we can speak, one of the first things that we are taught by our parents is the idea of right and wrong. This continues and intensifies when we go to school and experience particular codes of both good and bad behaviour. At some point, we will transgress these codes and appear to be guilty of some misdemeanour. This leads to us accepting the codes and norms of a group so that we will be accepted in turn by them. Although you may appear loyal and law-abiding to your group, it can often result in you being disloyal to some parts of your natural character.

24. CATCHING A TRAIN

Dream

You are rushing to the railway station because you have to catch a particular train. As you arrive at the station you may start to get anxious because you are unsure which platform to go to and can't remember where you put your ticket. You may arrive on the platform just in time to see the train disappearing into the distance. If you do make it onto the train you might start to worry whether you are on the correct train and actually going the right way, or become concerned about which station to get off at.

Meaning

When you dream of trying to catch a train, you are thinking about a specific career path you would like to follow in your waking life. Trains run along specific routes at predetermined times and so often symbolize particular career paths within a large organization. Different trains represent different career opportunities and train stations are ways of embarking on these opportunities. Your hope is that if you embark on this path and follow it for a certain amount of time, then you will reach a certain professional ambition. Trying to reach the correct embarkation point suggests that you are still trying to find the right platform for your career ambitions. Your ticket represents your opportunity to follow this path and you are concerned that you might lose it.

If you arrive on the platform and see the train disappearing into the distance, then you are concerned that you might lose the chance to get on board with a particular opportunity. Being on a train that won't stop indicates that you would like to change your current career path but you are finding it difficult because of commitments that you have made. Although it may seem as if your career is running on rails and everything is going well, it may be frustrating for you because you seem to be restricted to following a rigid path that you feel you can't escape from. Trains make regular stops, however, and these are opportunities for you to change career track.

Action

This dream is about choosing where you want to go in life and how you can get your ambitions on track. To successfully embark on your chosen career, you have to commit to go in a certain direction for a set amount of time. It may be difficult for you to make this commitment but keeping your options open might also mean that you miss this particular opportunity to get ahead. Although you may feel a bit trapped by routine, it is sometimes best just to sit tight until you reach your goal, rather than trying to make a risky career move.

Background

Many of us associate trains with commuting to work and they can provide us with a feeling of certain and steady progress, while giving the knowledge that we can't deviate from our chosen route. As we advance along our accepted path, we see stations as indicators of progress. This leads us to saying thing like *'having ideas above your station'*, if we think someone won't advance as far and achieve the status that they had hoped. If we deviate from this predetermined course, we end up using phrases such as *'going off track'* or that someone has *'gone off the rails'*.

25. BACK AT SCHOOL

Dream

Although you are an adult, you find yourself back at your old school for some reason. You are often re-sitting your final year and wondering why you have to keep turning up for lessons. Rather than go to classes, you are impatient to leave school so you can use your knowledge out in the real world. There may be one important class that you are attempting to attend but you keep getting lost as you make your way to the classroom where it is being taught. You often find that your old teachers are trying to make you pay more attention to specific issues.

Meaning

When you dream of being back at school or college, you feel that you have the opportunity to learn a valuable lesson in your daily life. Although school is usually associated with academic education, it also represents all the other information that you learn during your formative years. School is the place you enter as a child and leave as an adult and so it tends to symbolize your growing independence and your ability to deal with other people, especially those in positions of authority. Being back in your final year suggests that you are learning how to resolve a particular situation in your waking life in a mature and adult manner. You are impatient to do this because you are keen to assert your individuality.

The class you are trying to attend often indicates the nature of the lesson that you are learning in your daily life. A history lesson is urging you to let go of the past and move into the future. Geography lessons are about broadening your horizons and exploring unfamiliar areas. A language lesson suggests that you need to express yourself more fluently and in different ways. Maths lessons indicate that you need to be more rational and calculating as you work through a problem. Science classes are about basing your actions on solid evidence and art classes show you need to be more creative and individual. The teachers symbolize you listening to your older, wiser self.

Action

This dream is trying to teach you that you never stop learning, even after you have graduated from a formal educational environment. The more you learn about the world around you, the more you learn about yourself. This opens you up to greater self-awareness and a more fundamental realization of your potential in life. It can be tempting to skip these lessons but this usually results in being stuck in the same old patterns and self-limiting beliefs. No matter what subject you study, the fundamental learning outcome is always a deeper self-awareness.

Background

Our time at school is when we really begin to learn about the outside world beyond our homes. Away from our parents, we have to learn how to complete tasks within specified times and to independently negotiate relationships with other people. Our school experience is reflected in much of our working life where the professional lessons we learn often resonate with learning experiences we had as scholars. Although we no may no longer be assessed by formal examinations, we continue to examine our performance and judge our level of success.

26. CELEBRITY ENCOUNTER

Dream

You are surprised and delighted when one of your favourite celebrities approaches and begins chatting to you as if they have known you for years. You find yourself wanting to acknowledge their status by telling them what a big fan you are and how much you admire them. Your idol seems genuinely relaxed and comfortable in your company, and so you try and behave normally and just keep talking with them. Even though you start off feeling quite nervous and in awe, you soon find yourself at ease with them, and after a while you are planning joint projects and further meetings.

Meaning

When you dream about meeting a celebrity you are thinking about the unique aspects of your personality that you respect and admire the most. Celebrities symbolize particular creative talents and performance abilities, and they also tend to be powerful and resourceful with the freedom of choice to make their decisions. The celebrity you meet represents these aspects of your character, which you are becoming more aware of in your waking life. Whatever quality you associate most with the celebrity is the quality that you are now starting to recognize in yourself. Your increasing awareness of your creativity may initially come as a surprise to you but talent often grows naturally with no conscious decision to develop it in a particular way.

Although you want to acknowledge how much your talents have grown, it can often be difficult for you to accept recognition and appreciation from others. It often seems easier not to draw attention to your gifts and to think of talent as being something that other people have, but not you. As you become more relaxed and comfortable with your unique abilities, however, it becomes easier to share them with a wider audience. The more that you allow other people to praise and admire your talents, the more you can develop and nurture your abilities. If your celebrity encounter is romantic or sexual, then this shows that you are becoming intensely and intimately aware of your unique talents and skills.

Action

This dream is shining the spotlight on your hidden talents and encouraging you to develop your unrealized abilities. It can be tempting to think that only other people possess talent but you also have unique skills. Although many celebrities appear to have always been successful, they have had to work hard to develop their talents, too. Like a celebrity, you should display your talents rather than hiding them. The more you recognize your skills and abilities, the more recognized and celebrated you will become in your chosen area of expertise.

Background

As our ancestors explored their natural power, they always created stories about beings with superhuman and supernatural characteristics. These were initially pagan warriors and queens who became worshipped as gods and goddesses, and who then were further developed into deities in every creed and culture. As collective mythologies faded during the era of Enlightenment and rational scientific thinking became more

prevalent, we began to use people who were regularly in the public eye to represent these god- and goddess-like qualities. But rather than worshipping them in temples and shrines, we now celebrate their apparently other-worldly powers and resources in our mass media.

27. EARTHQUAKES AND ERUPTIONS

Dream

You are going about your everyday business when suddenly the ground starts to shake and cracks begin to appear in it. Roads are crumpling up, buildings are falling down and you are trying to escape the earthquake and get yourself and others to a place of safety. Volcanoes pouring molten lava out onto the streets, setting fire to all it touches, often accompany the earthquake. Everything around you is in complete upheaval and it may feel like the world is ending. There seems to be absolutely nothing you can do about it as you can only watch the events unfolding.

Meaning

When you dream of an earthquake or an eruption, there is usually some huge personal upheaval occurring in your life, which is really shaking you up. In waking life, you use the ground as a constant reference that you can always rely on for stability and support. Earthquakes occur, however, when two apparently stable areas become subject to great tension and stress. This can often happen when one area of your life is beginning to severely impact another area. It may be that your work life has started to affect your home life and this is causing a lot of unspoken friction for you. Like earthquakes, these hidden tensions can reach a sudden breaking point where everyone and everything around you seems at fault.

Volcanoes are common in earthquake dreams and reflect how your hidden stresses can cause you to erupt in rage. Although you have been trying to contain your mounting anger, you find yourself losing your head and blowing your top. Your pent-up fury and frustration come spilling out like a bubbling and spitting stream of molten lava and there seems to be absolutely nothing that you can do about it. Giving vent to your anger and frustration might seem destructive but it can also be a great source of creative energy if you can channel it properly. Rather than letting hidden stresses build up uncontrollably, try letting off steam by directing your energy into activities that really move you.

Action

To move on from this dream, it is best if you can find some way of releasing these feelings of frustration, which are bubbling away under the surface of your calm exterior. The most powerful way of channelling your emotions is just to express what you are feeling. There are probably some major stresses that really make you overheat, but it is best to start on some smaller issues and establish a channel for honest communication. You don't have to scream and shout, instead just calmly assert yourself, giving voice to your true feelings, until you feel your needs really are being met.

Background

Although we may never personally experience an earthquake or a volcanic eruption, they are regular occurrences that

are reported in the media and have mythological status in apocalyptic movies. These outer topographic events reflect a major change in our inner landscapes and the positions we hold. Much of our language concerning major personal change and the release of frustrations is based on fundamental reshaping of the landscape and the release of what usually lies under the surface. We speak of our *'world being rocked'*, *'an earthshaking experience'*, or someone *'blowing their top'*.

28. LOST OR BROKEN-DOWN CAR

Dream

You need to get to an important appointment but your car seems to have broken down. When you hurry out to where you parked it you are dismayed to find that it won't start. Even though it has been regularly serviced and well looked after, it just won't fire up and, as you walk around it, you may discover punctured tyres or that vital components are damaged or missing. You might also find that your whole car has disappeared. It may have been stolen or perhaps you just can't remember where you parked it.

Meaning

Dreaming of a lost or broken-down car usually signifies that you feel you have somehow lost your impetus and ambition in waking life. The vehicles that transport you in dreams reflect different ways of getting where you want to go in your life. A car is usually a personal vehicle and so it often represents your individual drive as you progress in your career. It can also reflect how much power and control you have as you try to achieve particular personal ambitions. Circumstances, however, can often result in you having to park some of your aspirations in the hope that you can return to them later and continue with your progress. An important appointment indicates a significant opportunity to fire up your ambitions again.

Having difficulty in starting the car suggests that you are finding it difficult to get fired up and motivated again. You may not have the same spark you once had or feel you don't have all the resources you need to fuel your ambitions. It may have seemed that you were maintaining your drive towards your goal but you now realize that you have been neglecting some vital areas. Punctured tyres suggest that you are feeling a bit let down and deflated and need to get pumped up again about your goals. If your car seems to have been stolen, then you feel that you aren't valuing yourself enough and this is preventing you from actively pursuing your ambitions.

Action

This dream is alerting you to a loss of your motivation and direction in waking life. Your drive can often fade away quite gradually if you do not maintain your underlying momentum and it can be quite a shock when you realize that it isn't there when you really need it. The most direct way of regaining your drive is to decide where you want to focus your energies. The more decisive and driving you can be, the easier it will be to coax the vehicle for your ambitions back into life and get your career back on the road.

Background

Our personal vehicles symbolize our ability to choose an objective in life and independently travel towards it. Prior to the

invention of the car at the end of the 19th century, it was more common to dream about a horse being sick or stolen. Those who live in cultures near or on water also dream of their boats sinking or being lost. The horse used to provide us with phrases such as *'having the bit between their teeth'* or *'having to rein in our ambitions'*. Now we tend to use phrases associated with cars such as *'running on empty'* or *'shifting up a gear'*.

29. DEATH OF A LOVED ONE

Dream

You are shocked and saddened to learn of the death of someone who you love dearly. The loved one is often one of your parents or someone who you could always rely on for unconditional love and support. Although you are devastated at the loss, you make a great effort to ensure that everyone recognizes the incredible qualities your loved one embodied during their life. You wake from this dream feeling incredibly sad but this turns to joy and relief as you realize your loved one is still alive.

Meaning

When you dream about the death of a loved one, it often symbolizes a definite ending of one way of life and the start of a new one. This isn't a precognitive dream that a loved one will die. When you dream of another person, you are usually using them to represent a characteristic personal quality of your own. If your loved one is warm and nurturing in waking life, you are considering your capacities for warmth and nurturing.

If your loved often seems responsible and capable, you are questioning your capabilities and responsibilities. The death of your loved one in your dream indicates that this particular quality that you possess is being transformed in some way.

This transformation is often the result of a major change in your waking life where you have to let go of old habits and welcome new ways of doing things into your life. This dream often takes place at a graveside because you are being encouraged to respectfully put the past to rest so you can move ahead into a new future. If the dream takes place in a hospital, it often indicates that you may have an unhealthy dependency on your loved one and need to be more responsible and self-reliant in your waking life. The joyful realization that your loved one is still alive emphasizes that your connection with them is being reborn and renewed, and will help you forge an even stronger bond with them.

Action

This dream is reassuring you that you are reaching the end of a particular period of activity in your life and affirming that a whole new area of opportunity is beginning for you. By releasing yourself from your past, you have the freedom to step into a new future. Although it may be intriguing to consider this dream as a premonition of an actual death, this is hardly ever the case. Instead of becoming concerned about a possible death, you should consider the new possibilities that are opening up for you, and how you can use them to enrich and expand your life.

Background

One of the first anxieties we experience as children is separation anxiety from our parents who are nurturing us and ensuring

our comfort and safety. We experience the parent leaving and then reappearing but it can be very worrying for us while they have gone. The more independent we become, the less we depend on our parents and loved ones. But when faced with uncertain situations, we always hope they will reappear and make everything all right again. Although death is often considered as an utter finality, it is a natural ending leading to new beginnings.

30. WRONG NUMBER OR BUTTON

Dream

You are trying to dial a number on your telephone but you keep getting it wrong. Although it may be a familiar number, you frustratingly keep pressing the wrong buttons, mixing up the last two or three digits. You really need to make this call because you have to speak to someone urgently. Even if you do manage to make the connection, you often find that you have dialled the incorrect number and have reached someone who you don't recognize. Similar dreams can occur where you are trying to send an important text or gain access to somewhere using a keypad entry system.

Meaning

If you dream that you keep getting a wrong number or are pressing the wrong button, then there is a situation in your waking life where you are finding it difficult to communicate with a particular person. Although you may routinely connect with this person, there seems to be a bit of a mix-up this time and you can't get your message across in the way that you would really like to. The telephone is usually associated with communicating words and messages but this dream is more about how you communicate by your actions and behaviours. You have a habitual way of dealing with this person and usually know the right buttons to press in order to make them respond in a particular way.

For some reason, however, they aren't responding to your frantic button-pushing this time and you just can't get through to them whatever you do. Even if you do manage to connect with them, they seem to be behaving in a way that you don't recognize. This usually indicates that the person is picking up on your behaviour and no longer responding to your requests. As you become more aware of this, it encourages you to reflect on your action by taking a deeper look at how you connect with others and how you connect with yourself. Dreaming of a keypad system or an important text usually indicates that you are thinking about how you act and behave in your workplace.

Action

The message this dream is trying to communicate is that dealing with a human being is different from trying to operate a machine. Not being able to get through to someone is often because of your communication style, rather than being the fault of the person you are trying to connect with. Instead of continually attempting to get your message across, listen to what the other person is really saying to you. The more that you are aware of their needs, the stronger your connection will be with them and the more likely they are to heed your messages.

Background

From the first time we turn on a light switch, we have the awareness of the cause and effect of our specific actions. When we start to use phones and computers, we know that we have to follow certain procedures in order to communicate with specific people. Much of our communication with others is remote rather than face-to-face, and so, instead of starting to communicate by seeing the other person and judging their mood, we press a series of buttons and express our feelings. This can often lead to a feeling of disconnection and misunderstanding.

31. ANGRY CONFRONTATION

Dream

Although you are normally a quiet and peace-loving person, you find someone raging and shouting at you in an angry confrontation. You are sure that the other person started the argument and you are just trying to defend your point of view as they rant and yell at you. Even though you aren't quite sure about the reasons for the dispute, you are becoming incredibly wound up and annoyed about it. The confrontation gets even angrier and louder, until you are sure that you are just about to explode with rage.

Meaning

If you dream of being involved in an angry confrontation, you are often confronting your feelings of frustration and annoyance in waking life. Although you are usually quite placid and peaceable, something has happened that has made you really angry. Your normal calm demeanour can make this very challenging for you because you aren't sure how to express your upset feelings. Your certainty that the other person started the argument indicates they have somehow triggered these feelings of frustration. But this was probably completely unintentional on their part and all they have really done is to reveal the deeper cause of your dissatisfaction. Realizing that your hidden frustrations are being exposed can also make you feel vulnerable and defensive.

Those who have become involved in an unpleasant situation through no fault of their own, and are finding it difficult to voice what their real needs are, often experience this dream. If you find your lover screeching at you in a rage, then there is some fundamental issue in your relationship in waking life where you feel your needs aren't being met. You feel, however, that it would be very destructive to voice what you really want to say to your partner. An angry boss usually symbolizes your seething frustration at their neglect of your talents. If a deceased person is shouting angrily at you, it does not mean that they are angry with you, but that you are angry with them for seemingly leaving you behind when they passed on.

Action

This dream is shouting out that you are in a situation you find really frustrating. You are finding it very challenging to give voice to your real concerns, however, and this is causing resentment to keep building up inside you. You are afraid to say what you really feel in case you upset other people but this is creating a lot of inner tension for you. Rather than

having to resort to screaming and shouting, try just calmly asserting yourself until you feel your needs are being really met.

Background

Some of the first lessons we learn about living as part of a polite and stable society are about containing our feelings, particularly seemingly destructive emotions such as anger. But feeling unable to express anger allows it to build up inside us and we start to project this tension into the outside world, seeing potential conflict in every encounter we have. Rather than just saying what is on our mind, our tensions become a chronic inner conflict that can absorb a lot of our energy, leaving us feeling defeated and powerless.

32. CAN'T FIND YOUR WAY HOME

Dream

You have been on a journey somewhere and really want to get home but for some reason you can't find your way back. Although you are sure you know the way home, everything in your surroundings appears really confusing. You keep trying different routes but they seem to take you further and further away from home rather than getting closer to it. Even though other people are trying to help you, they aren't able to point you in the right direction. You are usually alone and may be on foot or travelling in some kind of vehicle.

Meaning

When you dream that you can't find your way home, you feel that you aren't able to express who you really are in waking life. Your home represents your true self, who you really are when you feel most at home. Being on a journey somewhere shows that you have been going through a period of change and now you are moving on beyond it. Navigating these changes meant you had to behave in a way that felt appropriate at the time but no longer feels natural. This has left you frustrated about not being able to be yourself and can often happen in a job where you don't feel that you are doing what you really want to do.

It can also happen in a relationship where you feel that your contribution isn't being recognized or your needs aren't being met. The different routes you try are the different roles you assume in the hope of pleasing other people but this removes you even further from your self and needs. Although other people may try and suggest the direction you should take, you really have to choose your path. You are usually travelling alone because this is about your individual identity and how you can truly express it. The more personal your transport, such as being on foot or bicycle, then the more personal the area of your life that your dream is directing your attention towards.

Action

This dream is showing you the way to find out who you really are in life. It can be easy to immerse yourself in the lives and needs of other people but this can cause you to lose sight of your needs and deeper self. No matter how hard you work and how many sacrifices you make for others, you may always end up feeling unfulfilled and undervalued. The more honest you

are about declaring your purpose and needs to other people, the more at home you will feel with yourself.

Background

'There's no place like home' and it is the fundamental symbol of identity in dreams, being the place where we all want to return to when we need to relax and recover. Our home is a place where we can just be ourselves, protected from the demands and judgements of other people. The concept of a homeland also shows up in national identities, where the characteristics of people are attributed to the area of the world that they come from. Like a homeland, your home is where you come from and often contains the deepest roots of your identity.

33. PURSUED BY THE AUTHORITIES

Dream

An official-looking group of uniformed people are pursuing you as you desperately try to escape from them. You know they are definitely after you but aren't sure why. Your pursuers are most often men, usually dressed in black and they are strangers to you. They seem to be very well organized and will often be carrying weapons. You are really scared they will kill you when they finally catch you. No matter where you hide or how fast you run, they always seem to be getting closer as they pursue you relentlessly.

Meaning

If you dream about being chased by the authorities, it usually suggests that you have concerns about your freedom to act and your obligations as an individual in waking life. These dreams often start at a young age, as you try to establish your identity and freedom of action. As you try to negotiate your individual needs within the collective requirements of a larger group, it invariably causes tension with parents, teachers and other figures in authority. This tension can continue through your life as you attempt to balance your responsibilities with your need for freedom and self-determination. Although you may appear to be trying to escape your commitments, responsible people with a strong sense of duty most often experience this dream.

The people chasing you represent your sense of accountability and duty as you try to control your individual needs. They are part of you and you can't escape your sense of duty, no matter how much you try. Men tend to symbolize formal authority and represent your ability to give yourself permission to act in a way that you choose. It can seem strange to feel you have this power, and their black clothing shows that this realization is emerging from your unconscious awareness. Their size and organization reflects how well organized you can be. You are scared that your responsible attitude will kill your individuality but you have the ultimate authority for your behaviour.

Action

This dream is giving you permission to take responsibility and authority for your actions. It can be easy to blame other people for apparently limiting your freedom and preventing you from doing what you want to do. However, the more self-disciplined you are in taking responsibility for your actions, the more

freedom you will have in life. One of your greatest freedoms is being able to use your power responsibly. If you shirk away from your obligations to your needs, you will always feel that you are prey to the actions of others.

Background

Our first experience of authority is from our parents who try to teach us to be responsible and accountable for our actions. As children, we very often just want to act on impulse and run around enjoying ourselves as much as possible. It often seems as if authority restricts our freedom, particularly when we go to school, but what we learn gives us the opportunity to be free. As adults, we can sometimes think some institutions and authorities are trying to remove our freedoms and so we end up comparing them to fascist societies and totalitarian regimes.

34. CHILDHOOD HOUSE

Dream

Although you are an adult, you are visiting your childhood house, which you left years and years ago. It seems to be exactly the same way as when you left and you are often looking for something that you feel you left behind there. You may find yourself searching through old cupboards and wardrobes, particularly in your bedroom. Whatever you are looking for is often to be found under your old bed and you are delighted to find it. You might also discover yourself out in the garden playing with childhood friends and favourite toys.

Meaning

If you dream about visiting your childhood house, you are often reflecting on some formative experiences from your early years in life. A house usually represents yourself in your dreams and so visiting it suggests you are revisiting some of the fundamental influences that have helped to shape your identity. Although you have built upon many of these foundational experiences in your waking life, there may be other parts of your childhood identity you didn't have the chance to develop so fully. Your old house seems to be exactly the way you left it because these aspects of your character have remained unchanged. These individual qualities have been dormant all this time, waiting for the opportunity for you to fully express them.

As you search through your childhood house, you are usually trying to rediscover these qualities and reconnect with them again. The furniture often symbolizes all your individual habits and memories with the cupboards and wardrobes representing where you store your childhood experiences. Although you have had to tidy these memories away and keep them out of sight, you now want to bring them back out into the light of day. Your bed represents the place where you are most relaxed and comfortable with yourself, so finding something under there shows that you are rediscovering a key part of who you really are. Being in the garden with your friends and toys suggests that you are playing around with your newfound potential.

Action

This dream is encouraging you to explore undiscovered parts of your identity and to develop their true potential, now that you have the time and resources to do it. This particular area of your character is often a talent that you did not have the opportunity

or confidence to express when you were younger. It can be easy to continue to ignore this creative gift in adult life but it is a fundamental part of who you are. Making it become a reality will be a realization of one of your childhood dreams.

Background

We learn by analogy and we start to become aware that we are separate from the world around the age of two to three, when we realize that we have an inner and an outer world. We use our first house as an analogy for our self because it also has an inside and an outside, associating different parts with different aspects of our growing personality. As we grow we are often encouraged to leave part of our childhood life behind and this becomes symbolized in our unconscious as our childhood house.

35. UNABLE TO MOVE

Dream

You are being menaced by a presence that seems dark and evil, but you find yourself completely unable to move. No matter how much you try to wriggle and squirm, your body seems to stay exactly where it is. Sometimes you may feel as if a great weight is crushing down on your chest, making it difficult for you to breathe. It can also seem as if something or someone is wrapped around you and is squeezing and hugging you. You may also feel as if you are frozen and stuck in snow or ice.

Meaning

Dreaming of being unable to move can be an utterly terrifying experience, as it seems so desperately vivid and real. This apparent inability to change position is caused by a protective physiological function, which has evolved to prevent your body moving around when you dream. Instead of physically acting out your dreams, your brain blocks nerve signals to your limbs and torso. This creates the sensation of paralysis and is quite often a constricting feeling, as if there is a person or a weight pressing down on your chest. The nature of this physiological function means that sleep paralysis almost invariably occurs when you are dreaming. If you wake suddenly from a dream, you can feel paralysed with the dream imagery still lingering in your perception.

This can lead to a variety of hallucinations, particularly dark shadowy figures such as men dressed in black wrapping their arms around you or old hags sitting on your chest. The feeling of restricted breathing is caused by the contraction of your chest muscles. The more anxious you become during the experience, the more your muscles tense up and the worse it seems to get. Sleep paralysis usually occurs when you are going through some stressful situation in your waking life and you aren't receiving enough physical rest. The lack of rest means that you wake up physically tired but with a very active mind and this can trigger the experience; the feeling of coldness and freezing can be compounded by waking up in a cold sweat.

Action

If you wake up and feel unable to move, no matter how much you try, the best option is to attempt to just relax for a few

moments. Although this may seem counter-intuitive, relaxing lets your body wake up at its own pace and allows the feeling of terror to pass and fade away. To prevent sleep paralysis happening, you need to ensure that you are getting the highest quality sleep that you can. The best way to do this is to relax as much as possible before you go to sleep and try to avoid excessive alcohol, nicotine and unnecessary stress.

Background

We often think that the classic response to an unexpected and threatening situation is the so-called fight or flight response. Instead of fighting off potential danger or fleeing from it, however, our most common response is to freeze; by freezing and staying absolutely still, we hope that an assailant or attacker won't notice us. This natural response is something we automatically tend to do in the hypnopompic state between dreaming and waking where this condition is most often experienced. The figures we conjure up in our minds have passed into myth and legend as spirits of the night.

36. WINNING THE LOTTERY

Dream

As you check your lottery numbers, you suddenly realize that you have won the jackpot! You are so surprised that you check your numbers again and again to make absolutely sure of your success. You may also dream that you have stumbled upon a vast underground treasure hoard or found a huge suitcase

full of money. As you come to terms with your fantastic good fortune, you may start to become anxious about how to bank your winnings or bring the treasure safely to the surface and claim rightful ownership of it.

Meaning

When you dream of winning the lottery or finding treasure, you are becoming more consciously aware of a unique and valuable talent you possess. This burgeoning awareness is often triggered by an unexpected chance that you have recently encountered in your waking life. Although it may seem as if you are being suddenly presented with this opportunity without making any effort, the truth is that it could not happen without your unique abilities. Your talents may have been lying dormant for some time and this is your big chance to use them. Like the winning numbers on your lottery ticket it all seems to add up and make sense but you can find it difficult to accept your good fortune.

Finding a huge treasure hoard underground shows that you have a whole wealth of hidden talent. Although you know that you possess these abilities, it can be difficult to consistently bring them into the open and express them fully. Being anxious about claiming rightful ownership of your winnings or treasure indicates that you still lack confidence in your natural creative abilities. This self-doubt is probably why your gifts have remained concealed until this opportunity became apparent. The more confidence you have in your abilities and the more you accept the value of your talents, then the more likely you are to create opportunities for yourself, rather than just hoping for the best and waiting for fortune to smile on you.

Action

The value of this dream is that it shows you have some unique talents and skills that you need to treasure. It encourages you to explore and discover these hidden abilities and find ways of expressing them. The key to realizing the great value of your talents is to start celebrating your creative gifts, however minor they seem at the moment. The more you are aware of your abilities, the more chance there is that other people will recognize your real value. Rather than waiting to be discovered by others, start finding out what you can do if you really try.

Background

Some of the first stories that we hear are fairy tales about the quest for buried treasure and the discovery of untold riches. There are many myths and legends about rich and promised lands where the streets are paved with gold. In these stories, the treasure is often stumbled upon almost by chance and our modern version of this is the lottery. In the same way, we often hope that other people will serendipitously stumble upon our talents and discover us. The word talent is derived from the Latin *talentum*, meaning *'a unit of currency'* and we tend to equate our talents with financial success.

37. MISSING A PLANE

Dream

You arrive at the airport in a panic, knowing that you only have a few minutes to get through security and catch your flight. You

eagerly scan the departure boards to find your flight details but they seem to be all jumbled up with contradictory information. Even though you look around for someone to help you, no one is paying any attention to your predicament. You wish you had left home earlier to catch your flight but there were so many bags to pack and so much to do before you left. Your heart sinks as you hear your aircraft is departing.

Meaning

When you dream of missing a plane, you are becoming anxious that your plans aren't bringing you the fulfilment in daily life that you hoped they would. Aeroplanes are vehicles of the air and symbolize the ideas that soar through your boundless imagination. Trying to catch a plane suggests that you are hoping some of your ideas will take off and raise you up beyond the everyday world. Although you may panic, as you try to make the flight, you are probably well organized in waking life and have set some sort of a timetable for achieving your plans. You are feeling anxious because no matter how busy and how organized you are, you never seem to get any closer to realizing your highest aspirations.

Trying to get through security indicates that you often miss out on realizing your personal ambitions because you find it difficult to leave the security of your day-to-day existence. The jumbled-up information on the departure boards indicates that you are sometimes not entirely sure what would make you happiest in your life. You probably have a number of conflicting needs and these are pulling you in different directions. No one seems to recognize your predicament because you always seem so organized and so capable. All the bags you had to pack and all the things you had to do suggest that you spend most of your time looking after other people and not looking after your needs.

Action

The message from this dream is about securing the opportunity to put your ambitions into action. Although you have all sorts of timetables for your planned accomplishments, you are often disappointed when contentment and happiness don't arrive on schedule. This is often because you fill your life with busy activity rather than choosing specific and purposeful action to take you where you really want to be. Keeping yourself busy is often a way to avoid connecting with your higher purpose, and in order to get where you want to go, you will need to start exploring beyond the areas where you feel secure.

Background

The process of getting to the airport and embarking can often take longer than the flight itself. This often results in us feeling under constant time pressure to get onto the aircraft because there can be so many unexpected hold-ups and delays. Airliners also leave at certain times for specific destinations and are either waiting on the ground or travelling in the air so we use them to represent opportunities that have a finite time span. Before air travel, we used to dream about missing the tide, or particular natural events that favoured agricultural opportunities.

38. GRAVES AND CORPSES

Dream

You see something pale and white sticking out of a dark mound of earth and as you get closer to it, you are horrified to realize that you have stumbled upon a dead body. Even though you weren't involved in the death of the person, you feel extremely guilty and want to cover up the body somehow. As you try to bury it, you may find a number of other bodies previously interred in a mass grave. You hurry up and attempt to conceal the grave so you can escape before attracting any attention.

Meaning

When you dream about buried corpses you are usually considering your hidden abilities and thinking about how you can use them to bring a particular plan into life. Stumbling upon a dead body suggests that you have a unique ability that you have abandoned in the past. Although you thought your chance to use this talent was dead and buried, a new opportunity in your waking life has caused it to surface again, bringing it back out into the open. Even though it seemed inevitable, given your circumstances at the time, you still feel guilty about abandoning your most cherished hopes and dreams. This feeling of guilt and regret often makes you want to continue to cover up your talents.

You may have initially abandoned your particular creative passion in order to meet the expectations of other people. This was probably done in the shallow hope that they might accept and appreciate you, but all you have done is kill off your passionate creativity and conceal it superficially. What you are now uncovering is the embodiment of your unique talents and you have the opportunity to resurrect your ambitions. If you dream that you caused the death of the person, it was you who made the choice to abandon your talent. Dreaming of uncovering multiple bodies in a mass grave suggests you may have multiple opportunities to express your talents as part of a team.

Action

This dream is drawing your attention to your need to resurrect your neglected talent and bring it back to life. You unconsciously know that you are in grave danger of abandoning something that makes your life worth living, but you are consciously choosing to do this in the hope that you will fit in with other people and be accepted by them. No matter how deeply you try and conceal your unique abilities, they just refuse to lie down and will keep surfacing at inopportune moments. Rather than feeling guilty about your individual talents, try breathing some new life into them.

Background

Although most of us rarely encounter a lifeless body, the majority of our more popular stories involve murders and corpses, and the mysteries surrounding their demise. In these stories, one party is usually trying to conceal the body while the other is trying to find it and establish the cause of the death. This classic tale of the whodunnit resonates with our guilt at concealing our talents and our efforts to find out why we have ignored them. Although it may be a cliché that the culprit is usually the butler, we often neglect our own needs while trying to serve the needs of other people.

39. SPIES AND SECRET AGENTS

Dream

You have the uneasy feeling that spies or secret agents are covertly following you and, although you try to evade them, you seem to be kept under constant observation. Even though you try to rationalize your concerns, you suspect that your phone has been bugged and strangers are reading all your personal messages. You want to report these undercover activities to the authorities but are concerned they might be the people actually controlling your surveillance. It feels like you can trust no one and you remain ever vigilant as you attempt to stay one step ahead of your constant shadows.

Meaning

When you dream about being under constant surveillance by spies or secret agents, you are concerned about divulging your hidden sentiments in waking life. Secret agents usually symbolize sensitive emotions that you try to keep concealed from others, and spies represent how you reveal your real feelings in unguarded moments. This behaviour is often experienced when you try to force yourself to behave in a particular way by assuming an identity that disguises your true nature. Even though you are open and honest, this situation can occur when the real you is secretly rebelling, as you attempt to conform to the ideals and expectations of others. For example, during strict diets, you may find yourself renouncing the regime as you guiltily sneak the occasional biscuit.

Rather than admitting how you instinctively feel, you are constantly on guard as you selectively self-censor the emotions that you disclose to others. This can make you appear quite distant and you may often try to communicate in cryptic messages in the hope that other people on your wavelength will pick up on what you really mean. Apprehension about revealing a secret romantic crush, or any unique passion, is a common trigger for this dream. No matter how much you hide your true feelings, they keep leaking out as you clandestinely

pursue your undercover objective. Spies and secret agents are often depicted as powerful and seductive individuals, and reflect your developing confidence and charm as you become more adventurous and self-assured.

Action

This dream is helping you to uncover some of the hidden powers and passions that you usually tend to conceal. You may be shy about revealing sensitive feelings because you think it will compromise you in some way. It might seem like unfamiliar territory and you are concerned that disclosing some personal sentiments might provoke an adverse response from someone you want to be close to. Giving yourself permission to reveal some information about your special talents and true feelings, however, may prove a revelation for others and open up a whole world of new opportunities for you.

Background

Spies and secret agents are among our most popular fictional characters and usually they have permission to break the rules in order to achieve their objectives. As they pursue their vital missions to reveal the truth, they disguise their behaviour and adopt different identities. Their organizations are often based in secret headquarters, which echoes how you might consciously try to keep secret thoughts concealed in your head. From James Bond to Jason Bourne, we are fascinated by spooks and spies as they gather intelligence and uncover secrets that lead to clearer understanding of potentially valuable opportunities.

40. UNEXPLODED BOMB

Dream

You are shocked to stumble across an unexploded bomb. There may be a timing device counting down with flashing digital lights or a ticking alarm clock, and the bomb might be half buried in the ground. Sometimes the bomb is disguised and seems quite innocuous or there can be a big red button, inviting you to press it, and set the whole thing off. The bomb may be nuclear and be falling from the sky or arcing overhead in a destructive trajectory. Sometimes the bomb does explode and, although it destroys other things, it never seems to harm you.

Meaning

Dreaming about an unexploded bomb suggests that you have the potential chance to make a major transformation in your waking life. Bombs and explosives usually symbolize accumulated energy that you are concerned about releasing. This energy often builds up through continuing tension and frustration, with no apparent opportunity to release it safely and positively. Rather than being able to channel your anger productively, you are concerned that the whole situation is going to blow up in your face. The timing device counting down shows that your patience is running out and you feel that you might not be able to contain your dissatisfaction for much longer. The bomb being buried in the earth indicates that these frustrations are mainly of a practical nature.

Bombs dropping from the sky suggest you have a plan or an idea but are constantly being bombarded by setbacks and premature assumptions. Nuclear weapons indicate that you have the potential to liberate a huge amount of energy that would completely transform your life. You are anxious, however, that this release of energy would also be extremely destructive and involve lots of lingering issues, which might take a long time to resolve before you can move on. Even though you are keen to voice your frustrations, you are afraid that doing so will just backfire on you. The key to defusing the situation is to realize that it is your finger that is on the button and you have control of the situation.

Action

This dream is alerting you to the fact that you have a huge amount of potential energy available to you, which could positively change some aspect of your life and that you are currently repressing, or feel you have been forced to repress. You need to take control of your energy rather than waiting for it to be triggered by external events that you have no real control over. Instead of continually feeling that you are on a short fuse, try standing back and deciding where you can channel your energies most effectively.

Background

Much of our language around releasing our frustrations uses words and phrases associated with explosives such as *'if something doesn't happen soon, I'm just going to explode'*. We also use these phrases to celebrate the planned and channelled release of energy, saying someone is *'dynamite'* or that we are *'having an absolute blast'*. Although we usually associate explosions with sudden and unexpected bomb blasts,

explosives are used more often for constructive processes rather than destructive. From quarrying and tunnelling to construction projects, such as building dams, explosives are used to remove the old so that the new can be created.

41. WINNING AT SPORT

Dream

It has been a close-fought game and you feel a huge surge of elation as you realize you are winning. Although playing against your opponent has been a tough challenge, you have made a great effort and are starting to gain the upper hand in the competition. If you are playing in a team sport, then you are usually coordinating the rest of your side as you push forward to score more points. Even though you may not hit the winning shot, you are delighted by how the rest of the team are acknowledging your presence and appreciating your playing skills.

Meaning

When you dream of winning at sport, you are thinking about how you can maximize your performance and achieve your goals in waking life. Dreaming of competing in an individual sport reflects a personal challenge in which you are currently involved. Although it often seems as if you are competing against someone else in order to win a prize, you are actually challenging your doubts and fears about your ability to consistently perform. An individual win shows you are conquering these doubts and raising your game. The fact you

are having to battle to accomplish this task reflects the effort and commitment you are putting into achieving this particular result and highlights the uncertainties you have to deal with.

If you dream of participating in a team sport, then you are considering how you can achieve a common goal with other people. Although this group situation may involve your family and friends, it usually reflects a situation in your workplace where you are trying to achieve a collective success with your colleagues. The more you can act as a team player, then the more likely that you will be successful. A team sport can also indicate that you need to accommodate and reconcile competing aspects and needs of your personality. Participating in a particular sport suggests there are certain rules and regulations you have to observe in order for your accomplishments to be fully recognized by others.

Action

This dream is challenging you to resolve any doubts and fears you have about your performance. Although you know you have some winning strengths, you may also be concerned about certain areas that might make you feel vulnerable. Accepting and working with these vulnerabilities will help you to become stronger and to achieve even greater success. The key challenge you have to deal with isn't another person, but conquering your doubts and fears. In group situations, try working with other people rather than fighting against them, as this will help you to accomplish both your individual and collective goals.

Background

Play has always formed a large part of human activity. Although it may seem to have no real purpose, it is a vital method of

exploring new opportunities and testing out different scenarios. As play evolved, it became more structured and developed into more formalized games and sports. These sporting activities are one of the main ways that we evaluate our ability to perform and we often take our sports more seriously than we do work. Sportsmen and women provide inspiring examples of individuals and teams battling against adversity and overcoming huge challenges to win against the odds.

42. WEARING THE WRONG CLOTHES

Dream

You are out in public, usually on your way to an important meeting, when you realize that you are wearing the wrong clothes. Some of your garments may be normal, but parts of your outfit are missing or you are wearing one or two items of clothing that are entirely inappropriate for the occasion. It may be that you are wearing a colourful and extravagant hat with a sombre suit or perhaps you just feel that you have the wrong shoes on. You may also find yourself wearing someone else's clothes, which feel uncomfortable and don't seem to fit you properly.

Meaning

If you dream that you are wearing the wrong clothes in a particular situation, then you are anxious about how you might be appearing to other people in your waking life. Your clothes

often form the basis of how other people see you and we tend to choose our outfit according to the image that we want to present to others. If you want to appear formal and businesslike you might wear a smart suit and sensible shoes. If you are trying to identify yourself as being part of a large group of people, then you wear similar clothes to them, whether it is the latest fashion trend or an armed forces uniform.

What you wear is also an indication of your status and your identity, so wearing the wrong clothes can show that there is a mismatch between who you are trying to appear to be and who you really are. The type of missing or inappropriate clothing often indicates the nature of this discrepancy. If you are wearing the wrong hat, then you feel that your thinking is inappropriate or that you are in the wrong role. Wearing frivolous items of clothing, such as parts of a clown costume, suggest that you may not be taking things seriously enough. Wearing someone else's clothing, particularly another person's shoes, implies you feel you are trying be someone you're not. Badly fitting clothes show that you aren't fitting in, or perhaps you do not want to fit in.

Action

This dream is drawing your attention to the discrepancies between who you really are and how you feel that you are expected to appear. Rather than trying to behave in an unnatural way, which you hope will allow you to fit in, you need to consider how you might show up differently in particular situations. It can sometimes seem easier to disguise your talents but instead of conforming to other people's expectations of you, think about how you can display your individuality while respecting the nature of the circumstances that you find yourself in.

Background

Human beings started to wear clothing about 70,000 years ago and its original function was to protect us from harsh environments and the vagaries of climate. It wasn't long, however, before clothes became a symbol of status and affiliation within particular groups, and what we wear has now evolved from simple protective garments into a huge range of items that declare our identities. Although we may like to keep some parts of our identity under wraps, we often reveal these parts of our unspoken characters at fancy dress parties and during a variety of traditional celebrations.

43. STARRING IN A MOVIE

Dream

Although you were sure that you were just doing something quite ordinary, you suddenly realize that you are starring in a movie. You are the central character in the story and your co-stars and the other performers seem to be accepting you wholeheartedly. Although the director may be giving you some guidance, you speak your lines without hesitation and you know how the plot will unfold. The story is usually quite epic and you are enjoying being the centre of attention. You may also be presenting on television and are confidently talking to camera without any need for a script.

Meaning

Dreaming that you are performing in front of the camera often reflects that you are starting to see the bigger picture in your waking life. This dream suggests that you usually spend much of your time looking after other people and often do a lot of work behind the scenes in order to make sure everything runs smoothly and successfully. Being the central character in a movie, however, shows you are now beginning to turn your attention to your needs and how you can live the life you always wanted. Having the leading role in a movie symbolizes that recognizing and displaying what you have achieved already in your life will play a major part in realizing your long-term ambitions.

As you begin to recognize your achievements in waking life, you usually start to become a lot more confident in yourself. This sense of self-assurance gives you a definite direction and usually encourages other people to acknowledge and appreciate you far more easily. Rather than waiting for other people to tell you what to do, you know what needs to be said and done, and are happy to just take action yourself. Seeing this wider view also shows you have the resources and experience to create a different story from the one you are living presently. The director in the movie is your innate wisdom and is encouraging you to perform confidently using talents or skills you may have been neglecting.

Action

This dream is shining the spotlight on the fact that you are the main character in your life story, not just an extra in someone else's drama. Rather than waiting for other people to decide what they want to do, you need to be the person who initiates the action

and calls the shots. The more you can direct your efforts towards a unique purpose, the less direction you will need from other people. You also need to make sure your talent is recognized and that others always credit your role in their success.

Background

One of the most dreamlike experiences we can have is sitting in a darkened cinema, completely absorbed in the action unfolding right in front of us. In the same way the film projector shines out the characters onto the big screen, we project our identities and needs onto the characters in the movie. The film stars we identify with become mythical representations of our characteristics and show us how we might bring our unique qualities to light. The action on the screen reflects our stories and how we can achieve the happy endings we really desire.

44. BEING SHOT OR STABBED

Dream

An assailant is pointing a gun or a knife towards you, and you are shocked to find a bullet or blade suddenly piercing your body. Even though you are busy trying to stem the flow of blood pouring from your wounds, you try to ask your attacker why they want to harm you so badly. You attempt to escape in case you are shot or stabbed again but your attacker pursues you, threatening to attack you further. Although there seems to be no way you can defend yourself, you find you can still function and move despite your wounds.

Meaning

If you dream of being shot or stabbed, it often points to the fact that you feel you are being forced to do something against your will in waking life. Guns and knives usually represent someone asserting their power and threatening you with unpleasant consequences if you do not comply with their wishes. The bullet from a gun usually symbolizes the wounding effect of some particular action that you feel is being taken against you. Guns tend to be more impersonal and are used at greater distances than knives, so this usually indicates that you are feeling under threat in a professional relationship. Knives are used at closer range and being stabbed suggests that you are feeling cut up about a conflict in one of your personal relationships.

Although the bullet hole or stab wound may be distressing and painful, you are usually far more concerned about the motive, rather than the actual injury itself. It may seem as if the attack was completely unprovoked but this usually reflects a situation in your waking life where you may be behaving like a victim and making yourself an easy target for the frustrations of others. By refusing to defend yourself, you leave yourself open to all sorts of sniping criticism and back-stabbing. Trying to escape from this situation shows that you are finding it difficult to confront aggression and so others will continue being aggressive towards you. The best way to defend yourself is by having the courage to deflect unwarranted criticism by asserting your needs.

Action

The message from this dream is that you are allowing another person to assert their power over you and are doing nothing to stop them. Although you may feel powerless, this is often because you are scared of stepping into your power and

asserting what you really need. You will usually have to be quite blunt as you assert yourself and make sure that your needs are actually recognized. The more confidently you can stand up for yourself, the less likely it is that you will be seen as an easy target by others who want to take advantage of your openness.

Background

The main use of weapons is to remove someone's influence or to force them to behave in a particular manner. Guns and knives are personal weapons and so have come to symbolize an individual forcefully asserting their power over someone else. Although these weapons are relatively rare in normal waking life, their presence is ubiquitous in many of our films and stories. From classic Westerns to the latest murder mysteries, unwilling victims are subjected to the demands of gun- and knife-wielding attackers. This theme is continued in the latest shoot 'em up computer games where the player's success often depends on their skills with virtual weaponry.

45. TAKING THE WRONG ROUTE

Dream

You were sure that you knew where you were trying to get to but somehow it seems as if you are going the wrong way to get there. Even though you are extremely keen to reach your chosen destination, you panic as you realize that your current route is taking you further and further away. You want to change your direction but you don't seem to have any control

over where you are going because none of the roads seem to lead to your objective. You look around for ways to slow down or stop so you can resume your intended direction.

Meaning

When you dream of taking the wrong route, you feel you aren't progressing towards the objectives you would really like to achieve in your life. You thought that following this particular path might enable you to advance your ambitions but your goals just seem to be getting further and further away. You may feel that you have the freedom of choice to follow the direction you wanted to but your decision is often influenced by circumstances or by peer, or parental, pressure. Even though your path may seem predictable, safe and socially acceptable, you are starting to realize that it isn't a life path that you want to follow. This often results in you living a life that is expected of you rather than the one you want truly to live.

After making a commitment to this particular path you begin to realize, however, that it isn't particularly satisfying and will never bring you the fulfilment you need. Even though you would like to stop, making the choice to halt seems an even bigger decision than your original commitment to starting on your current path. It can seem easier and safer to keep doing what you are doing rather than risk changing direction. Like many well-worn pathways, it is easy to get into a rut that you feel that you can't get out of. It can also be difficult to slow down because you don't want all your commitments to start piling up in front of you.

Action

The message from this dream is that your desire to please other people is preventing you from getting to where you really want

to go in your life, and so it is worth reflecting on who or what is really driving you to succeed. Instead of thinking about what is acceptable to others, start to consider what your true life purpose is, because having a purpose is far more powerful than just having a plan. Plans can be thwarted by the unexpected but a purpose will always give you the fundamental motivation to achieve what you really want to in life.

Background

Destination and destiny are derived from the Latin word *destinare* which means *'to choose where you want to go by establishing your purpose'*. A destination is usually considered to be a physical location but most of the journeys we make are about fulfilling what we consider to be our individual destinies in life. Although our ancestors may have considered their lives to be predestined, our contemporary cultures give far more choice in discovering our true purpose and providing ways to fulfil it. The more you remain true to your purpose, the clearer and more certain your destination will become.

46. FORGOTTEN BABY

Dream

You are horrified to discover a baby that you gave birth to years ago, but had forgotten all about until now. The baby is usually found in a drawer or a cupboard when you are looking for something else. Even though you have apparently neglected the baby for years, it is still alive and you immediately begin to

take care of it and nurture it. You can't believe you abandoned your baby all that time ago and feel incredibly guilty and remorseful. The baby usually responds to your revitalizing love and care, and is soon healthy and thriving.

Meaning

When you dream about a forgotten baby, you are remembering a labour of love you created a while ago but had to abandon for some reason. The baby symbolizes a very precious part of you and represents a unique ambition or talent you possess. You have been ignoring this talent and now it is crying out to get your attention in waking life. Although you can't believe that you had completely forgotten about your baby, you realize you had to abandon this great gift of yours due to the circumstances you were in at the time. You wrapped your unique talent up and put it to one side, or stored it in a safe place in the hope that you could return to it sometime soon.

As your life continued, however, other priorities and responsibilities came along and your baby was left forgotten and neglected. When you laid it aside, for whatever reasons, you did it in the hope that you would one day return to it. Although the baby may now seem emaciated or ugly, it is still alive and kicking, and has the potential to grow into something healthy and wonderful. You feel guilty that you have neglected this precious part of yourself but it is never too late to explore your forgotten potential by rediscovering this love from the past. This baby is a seed of your fertile imagination that you brought into life and now you can encourage it to grow and thrive.

Action

This dream is calling out to tell you that you possess some fantastic skill or talent but that you may have been neglecting

it over the years. It may be easy to justify ignoring your deeper needs due to all the other demands you have had on your time but now you have the opportunity to devote some precious time to developing your unique talents. Even though it might take some time for you to build up your expertise again, you have a natural creative capacity that you need to nurture and develop into something utterly personal.

Background

The bond between parent and child is one of the strongest and most intuitive relationships. Babies are born helpless and the parent is responsible for taking care of them until the child is able to look after itself. This bond means a parent will sacrifice almost anything to ensure the baby's wellbeing. We also describe ideas that are very close to our hearts, as being *'our babies'* and can feel we are abandoning our deeper needs if we neglect these plans. Our creativity can often move us deeply in the same way that we are profoundly moved by the new lives that we create.

47. LIFE-THREATENING ILLNESS

Dream

Someone close to you has been diagnosed with a life-threatening illness and although they seemed healthy enough, you are shocked at the news. It may be that the illness is quite obvious in the form of a cancerous tumour or the person has become ill and frail, perhaps with a heart problem or other potentially

terminal condition. Although the illness seems incurable, you are hoping for a miracle and are trying to find some health professionals to take care of them. You may have the illness yourself even though you know that you are completely healthy in waking life.

Meaning

When you dream of a life-threatening illness you are usually involved in an emotionally unhealthy situation in your waking life. This is often a state of affairs that is making you feel ill at ease, but you think has no obvious remedy. You may have been managing to cope with your current condition for a while now but you have suddenly realized that you just can't go on like this any more. If the illness is in the form of a cancer, then the diagnosis is that some situation in your life is growing out of control and is beginning to intrude into other aspects of your life. This uncontrollable growth may feel as if it is sapping your energy and really eating you up inside.

If the ailment is a cardiac problem, then you are probably involved in a relationship where your heart isn't really in it. Rather than just being an incurable romantic and causing yourself unnecessary heartache, the healthiest option may be to explore other ways of expressing your love. Stomach complaints suggest that you feel that your circumstances aren't bringing you the fulfilment you had hoped they would. Instead of trying to just stomach the situation, try savouring some other ways of satisfying your ambitions. Wasting diseases usually reflect that you feel you are just wasting your talent and squandering opportunities. Although you hope that everything will suddenly just get better, the best remedy is to take some positive action yourself.

Action

The diagnosis from this dream is that you are in an unhealthy situation. Like the human body, your hopes and aspirations have a fantastic capacity to regenerate themselves but you are placing yourself in chronically stressful circumstances and not allowing this healing to occur. It may seem like you have no other options and an unhappy outcome is inevitable but there are always alternative ways to regain a healthy balance in your life. The more you take responsibility for your wellbeing, the healthier your outlook will be.

Background

Although we may not have actual personal experience of a life-threatening illness, many of our prime-time television dramas are set in hospitals or doctors' surgeries. Very often these dramas are about life-threatening illnesses where some situation has to be transformed dramatically in the patient's life so they can become whole and healthy again. The word *'heal'* comes from the Old English *haelan*, meaning *'to make whole'* and we hear this in the phrase *'being hale and hearty'*. Feeling truly healthy is often about taking positive action that makes us feel really whole.

48. LOSS OF A VALUABLE

Dream

You have lost something that is very valuable to you, and although it may be an object of high monetary worth, it might also have

a huge sentimental value for you. The missing item is often your purse or wallet and you only notice it is gone when you have to pay for something. As well as the value of its financial contents, it may also contain your identification and licences. You can't believe you were careless enough to lose it and you may become convinced that your valuable has been stolen.

Meaning

When you dream about losing something valuable, you are often considering how much you value yourself and how much you feel valued by others in waking life. The loss of your valuables indicates that you unconsciously feel that your self-worth has been diminished in some way and you are uncertain of how to restore your previous levels of healthy self-esteem. These feelings are usually triggered by a change in personal circumstances where you feel that your value isn't being acknowledged or appreciated the same way any longer. This can often happen where there has been a change in your financial circumstances or you no longer have the commitment and support of someone who was once close to you.

You know deep down inside that you are valuable person but your annoyance at not having your purse or wallet to pay for something reflects your frustration in not having your value recognized by other people. The loss of your identification and your licences suggests your lack of confidence is preventing you from taking part in activities that you really used to enjoy. Being convinced that your valuable has been stolen indicates you feel that other people have robbed you of some future opportunities and so are responsible for your loss of self-worth and status. You, however, are the person who has ultimate responsibility for maintaining your sense of self-esteem by ensuring that your real value is truly recognized by others.

Action

This dream is helping you to recover an enduring sense of self-worth and is re-establishing your ability to display your fundamental value to other people. In the same way that you would retrace your steps when looking for something that has been lost, it is valuable to reflect on your situation and put events into a wider perspective. Instead of blaming others for your circumstances, use this change to develop some new opportunities. The best way to feel invaluable again is just to be yourself and so rather than trying to impress anyone else, concentrate on what you value most about yourself.

Background

We often measure our success by the apparent value of the objects we accumulate because valuable items are often seen as a tangible reflection of our self-worth. The object itself is often not all that valuable, however, and can usually be replaced by another. The item may not actually contain anything meaningful or magical but only reflects the value that we give to it as we shine our self-esteem onto it. What makes the precious item so apparently valuable is the feeling of self-worth it inspires in us.

49. STALKED BY A PREDATOR

Dream

You are sure that an animal or creature is following and watching you. It alarms you to realize that a dangerous predator such as a big cat is stalking you and getting ready to pounce. This predator is often a lion, which appears in a familiar place such as your workplace or the street where you live. You may also find yourself being stalked by a tiger but only catch brief glimpses of your predator as it follows you. Sometimes a black panther might loom out of the shadows and startle you before it fades away into darkness again.

Meaning

Dreaming about being stalked by a predator suggests that you are concerned about becoming consumed by a part of your character that seems dangerous and uncontrollable to you. Animals usually symbolize your instinctive and untamed impulses and you are trying to control these in waking life by keeping your feelings in check. But no matter how much you try to tame and ignore them, your emotions always seem to be lurking in the shadows, ready to pounce in those unguarded moments when you are feeling most vulnerable. This anxiety about falling prey to your feelings often means you are reluctant to enter into new and unknown situations. The type of animal that appears in your dream represents the nature of these instinctive impulses.

If a lion is stalking you, then you are unsure about confidently displaying your pride in your talents. Even though you are very confident in your abilities, you feel that other people are ready to pounce on any mistakes you might make. Tigers usually symbolize a fierce independence and so a tiger hunting you down suggests you are very keen to assert your individuality but are concerned you might appear too aggressive and unapproachable. A black panther represents the stealthy power of your unconscious needs and being shadowed by a panther indicates you may feel powerless to control your underlying motivations. Other predators such as bears or wolves can show your concerns about protecting people close to you.

Action

This dream is making you aware that you are being too timid about displaying your instinctive abilities to other people. You are scared that your behaviour might become uncontrollable and others will reject you for being too dangerous and disruptive. Although your instincts have the potential to create havoc, they also have the ability to track down opportunities you might otherwise miss. Rather than trying to cage your instincts, start tracking your impulses and observing your behaviours. The more aware you are of your natural behaviour, the more confidently you can display your true nature.

Background

Although most of us don't have to deal with dangerous predators on a day-to-day basis, we are familiar with stories about lions, tigers, panthers and other beasts of prey. From a young age we are introduced to tales such as *The Jungle Book* and *The Lion King*. Most of us have a continued fascination for wildlife documentaries where we can see these large predators living their tooth-and-claw existence. We attribute particular qualities to these animals, with such phrases as a *'pride of lions'* or describing someone who is uniquely assertive as a *'tiger'*.

50. SPOOKY ATTIC

Dream

There has been something unusual happening in your attic and you aren't quite sure what is occurring up there. It is almost as if there is something spooky going on. You hear floorboards creaking when you know there shouldn't be anyone in the attic, you hear murmuring voices and sometimes all the stuff stored in there seems to rearrange itself in odd ways. You are scared to go in there in case you encounter a ghost, but you know that you will have to investigate it sometime soon to give yourself peace of mind.

Meaning

When you dream about an attic, you are often thinking about some of your memories and ideas in waking life. Different rooms in a house represent different aspects of your character and since attics are to be found at the top of houses, they tend to symbolize what is happening in your head. The attic is often used as a storage space and the contents tend to reflect plans and projects you have stored away for future use. These are often ideas you have had to abandon in the past because of your circumstances at the time. But something has now happened in your waking life, which has brought these plans back into mind, and is making you restless to explore them.

The creaking floorboards are steps you need to take to bring your ideas back to life and the voices you hear are the thoughts you would really like to express to others. The attic contents rearranging themselves show that you are playing around with different permutations of your ideas and reorganizing them into new and innovative plans. Exploring your hopes and ideas from the past can feel scary because it brings to mind all the people you could have been, and all the things you hoped to have achieved in your life. Although you thought you had abandoned these hopes, you have been storing them away in your headspace, waiting for the right opportunity to use them.

Action

The message from this dream is that you are becoming aware of some old thoughts and ideas that are starting to come back into your mind. You may have completely forgotten about these ideas but something has triggered them and brought them back to life. Rather than closing the door on them and hoping they will just fade away, try opening yourself up to the possibilities they might bring. It may seem difficult to give form to your thoughts and flesh them out but the more that you explore and understand them, the more tangible they will become.

Background

We often use a house to symbolize our self in dreams, and the space at the top of the house is used to represent the headspace at the top of our bodies. Like an attic, we often consider our head as a storage place where we keep things that we hope to use someday. In the same way that we rediscover possessions stored in a loft, we often talk of *'dusting down an idea'* or *'bringing a plan out into the light of day'*. The word *'attic'* can also refer to the epitympanic recess, the small upper space of the middle ear.

51. INSURMOUNTABLE OBSTACLE

Dream

You are trying to reach a particular objective but there always seems to be a seemingly insurmountable obstacle blocking your way. This barrier can be a natural feature like a wide turbulent river or a high imposing cliff, or perhaps a massive chasm or impenetrable forest. An object like an impassable wall or a locked gate can also prevent your progress. As you try to surmount the obstacle, you are often filled with feelings of powerlessness and anxiety. Even though you try to skirt around the barrier, it seems to stretch impossibly far in every direction with no flaws in its defences.

Meaning

When you dream of an insurmountable obstacle, there is some constant frustration in your waking life that seems to be limiting your forward progress. You may not experience this frustration every day, but it always holds you back in some way. Although the barrier appears to be external and physical, it is often a manifestation of some limiting belief you have about your abilities. This lack of self-belief is often rooted in a discontinuity or upset you experienced in your life. If the barrier is a river, it is probably an emotional upset and if it is a chasm, it is your way of thinking that is stopping your progress. A cliff or a wall often indicates that you feel you lack the resources to proceed.

Even though the obstacle seems to be obstructing your progress, it is also a barrier that you can hide behind when you are feeling vulnerable. Rather than the obstruction preventing you from stepping into the future, it becomes a rigid self-defence against all the anxieties and concerns that prevent your future progress and fulfilment. Your attempts to skirt around the obstacle reflect how you attempt to skirt around this frustration in your waking life. Rather than approach the obstacle head on, you have evolved a coping mechanism that helps you to deal with it. This coping mechanism will only get you so far, but breaking through the barrier of self-limitation is usually far more effective in taking you to the other side.

Action

The message from this dream is that you may need to tackle this particular issue as soon as possible. Although it may seem completely impenetrable, the key line of weakness is where you feel most strongly about the situation. Rather than dwelling on your weaknesses, use the strength of your feelings to actually declare what is holding you back. By putting your frustrations into perspective, the obstacle facing you will begin to shrink proportionately as well. As the obstruction diminishes into a manageable challenge, you will be able to move beyond it into a whole new area of opportunity.

Background

We often describe our inner worlds in terms of the physical landscapes that we journey through in our outer worlds. When we encounter barriers to our thinking or emotional obstacles, we use phrases like *'hitting the wall'*. The language we use when coping with these inner obstacles is usually also physical in nature, giving rise to phrases like *'I'll cross that bridge when*

I come to it'. By expressing our inner worlds in terms of outer-world topography, we can share where we feel we are at and offer ways forward to overcome potentially limiting obstacles.

52. INAPPROPRIATE INTIMACY

Dream

You find yourself trying to make love in very strange circumstances or surroundings. It may be that you are trying to be physically intimate in a public place and, although you feel embarrassed and exposed with far too many people around, no one else seems to notice. You may have found what seems to be a secluded spot, but other people keep interrupting you with the most trivial of excuses and distractions. You may also be making love in your workplace with a colleague who you don't find remotely attractive in waking life or making love while doing something else completely mundane.

Meaning

When you dream of making love in unusual surroundings, there is something unexpected happening in your waking life that is encouraging you to become more aware of one of your uniquely exciting talents. Dreaming of making love isn't usually about wish fulfilment but almost invariably about coming to a more intimate understanding of your abilities. Trying to make love in public suggests you would rather develop this exciting new skill in private, instead of working on it in public where you feel vulnerable and exposed. It may feel inappropriate to experience this level of excitement in a public situation, such as your workplace, but the fact that no one seems to notice indicates everyone is confident in your particular talents.

Even when you try to create some space to absorb and explore your growing awareness, you may find yourself constantly interrupted and intruded upon. This shows that you aren't giving yourself enough time and space to develop your new talent and to become familiar with how you can best make use of it. The colleague who you are making love with might not be attractive to you in waking life but they possess characteristics that you deeply and unconsciously admire. These aren't romantic qualities but professional capabilities, or the aptitude to deal with particular situations. These overwhelming feelings of excitement and amazement transcend any routine feelings that you might have, as you become more intimate with your abilities.

Action

The message from this dream is that you are beginning to reach a much greater awareness of some unique part of your character. You usually conceal this aspect of yourself because it seems so deeply personal and you aren't really sure how to handle it. As your awareness grows, however, you find yourself unable to contain your excitement and passion for your new abilities. Rather than trying to censor how you express your talents, try creating some private time and space for yourself, so that you can begin to gain a more intimate understanding of how best to use your abilities.

Background

The act of making love is also known as procreation and is intimately connected with the creative process. When we

get excited about new plans and projects, we speak about *'conceiving ideas'* and *'bringing them to life'*. This ability to create something unique can be especially thrilling, particularly at the conceptual stage, where the possibilities seem endless. The creative process can become an all-consuming passion for people who need to express themselves at a deeper and more intimate level. Creating something special, however, often requires the creators to open up to some of their vulnerabilities and inhibitions.

53. LIFE OR DEATH BATTLE

Dream

You are locked in a life or death battle with some powerful and dangerous adversary. No matter how hard you kick and punch, your enemy seems to match your every move and you find yourself becoming more and more desperate to overpower them. It seems to you that the only possible outcome of the battle is either your death or the death of your opponent. Your attacks on your adversary, however, often seem to have no effect and your opponent spends most of their time laughing at your pitiful efforts.

Meaning

Dreaming of being involved in a life or death battle can indicate that you are being faced with a situation in your waking life that seems to be a threat to your very existence. This perceived threat is often quite trivial in reality and the feeling of life or death is usually caused by your feelings of vulnerability. You often feel that you need to win every argument, no matter how small, in order to protect the more sensitive aspects of your character. Even though you like to present a strong and robust image in daily life, a part of you often feels weak and defenceless. You are desperate to protect this vulnerable area because you feel others might exploit your apparent weaknesses.

The reason your adversary matches your every move, no matter how much you fight and struggle, is because you are actually locked in an inner conflict with your self. Instead of appreciating your talents and skills, you spend all your time trying to protect what you perceive as your character flaws. You are desperate to destroy your weaknesses but, in the process, you ignore your strengths and end up feeling even weaker. The battle you are fighting isn't to destroy these chinks in your armour but to accept them. Your wiser self understands this, which is why it is so amused at your attempts to make yourself appear completely invulnerable to any threats.

Action

This dream reinforces the fact that you always put in your maximum effort as you attempt to achieve your goal. You need to ask yourself if you are applying your effort in the right areas and what force you are actually fighting against. Some of the most powerful fighting methods are Eastern martial arts and these rely on acknowledging the strength of your adversary and using it against them. A key part of this discipline is accepting your flaws and vulnerabilities, and the more that you accept your weaknesses, the stronger you can become.

Background

All our creeds and cultures have foundational stories involving heroes and heroines engaging in battles to the death with seemingly all-powerful adversaries. Although these stories started off as actual accounts of real battles, the life or death battle soon became ritualized in our games and sports. This became prevalent in Roman gladiatorial culture and has now become even more sanitized in our modern-day activities such as boxing and martial arts. These life or death battles now also form the basis of the most popular computer games, where the status and success of a player is determined by how many virtual opponents they eliminate.

54. MOUTH FULL OF CHEWING GUM

Dream

Your mouth is full of a sticky gooey substance like chewing gum. The more you chew it, the more it seems to expand and fill your mouth. Although you desperately want to spit it out, you can never seem to get rid of it. You may try to pull it out with your fingers but it just ends up in a sticky mess of bubbles. It can make you feel anxious that the gum might pull out your fillings and damage your teeth. You feel the gum might choke you if you swallow it and make you feel ill.

Meaning

If you dream that your mouth is filled with chewing gum, there is something you really need to say in your daily life but are having some difficulty expressing. When you dream of eating food, it symbolizes an activity in your waking life that will bring you the deeper fulfilment you need. Endlessly chewing gum suggests that you seem to be involved in a particular activity that absorbs much of your energy but isn't something you find ultimately fulfilling. This activity is often something that you do for someone else. Although it was initially stimulating, it soon lost its excitement and now has become a dull chore that makes you feel as if you are just going through the motions.

You would like to voice your concerns but worry it will cause a really sticky situation if you actually say what is on your mind. You may spend a lot of time chewing this over as you consider the most equable way of dealing with it. Even though it may have started off as an apparently small issue, it now appears to have become blown out of all proportion. Your teeth represent your personal power and you are worried this will be damaged if you try and bring everything out into the open. The best way for you to release your frustration, however, is to say what is on your mind by just spitting it out!

Action

This dream is encouraging you to express an opinion that you are finding difficult to say aloud. Although you may be gracious and articulate, you find it quite challenging to put your feelings about this situation into words. Your natural tendency is to sugar coat what you need to say in order to avoid any tension or discomfort. The more that you avoid saying what you really

want to, however, the more likely you will remain stuck in the same place. Speaking the truth will give you a taste of who you really can be.

Background

Many people, particularly dentists and orthodontists, associate the chewing-gum dream with grinding teeth. Their view is the chewing sensation is caused by tooth grinding and therefore is the cause of the dream. The reverse is actually true. Tooth grinding is usually experienced when a person is finding it difficult to express their true feelings. The same issue in waking life, which is generating the chewing-gum dream, also causes the dreamer to grind their teeth. Both the chewing-gum dream and tooth grinding usually cease when the person resolves the situation by expressing what they really need to say.

55. STUCK IN MUD

Dream

You seem to be stuck in a swamp and are finding it really difficult to move your legs. The swamp is usually mud and water but you can also find yourself mired in another sticky, viscous liquid such as quicksand or custard. You may have started off on solid ground but are just sinking down into it now. It can often feel as if you are leaning forward, able to move your head and arms but not your legs. The more you try to move, the more stuck you feel and it requires enormous effort to make any progress.

Meaning

When you dream, your legs represent your fundamental drive in pushing yourself forward through your life. If you feel that your legs are stuck then there is something impeding your progress in waking life. Rather than being a specific barrier, which prevents you from moving forward, a swamp of gooey liquid reflects a wider situation that is holding you back in some way. Liquid in a dream usually mirrors your emotions so even though you thought you were on solid ground, this situation is giving you a sinking feeling. Although mud is encountered most often, you may also find yourself wading through treacle or custard. This suggests that you may have thought that you were in quite a pleasant situation but now you feel a bit trapped.

Your current circumstances are usually caused by a lack of emotional clarity and certainty. Although you want to move forward, you feel you are bogged down in a messy and unresolved emotional situation, which is holding you back. To resolve this particular set of circumstances, you need to stop wallowing around in your emotions and take a firm line on where you stand. The clearer you are about your position, then the more quickly you can start moving forward. Your head may be leaning forward because you can theoretically see what needs to be done but no matter how much you theorize, nothing will happen until you take some practical steps to move forward out of this sticky situation.

Action

The message from this dream is that you need to do less thinking and more practical work to get yourself moving. Rather than theorizing about how things could be, you need to start putting some of your plans into action. Don't try to do

it all at once, just start off one small step at a time. These initial steps will probably require a bit of effort and it might be easy to give up because you think you aren't getting very far. The more momentum you can build up, however, the more easily you can step into your new future.

Background

Even with all our mechanized transport and modes of travel, our primary source of motion is still our legs and much of our language around progress is leg-based. We use phrases such as *'time is marching on'*, *'the steps we have to take'* and *'running it past someone'*. When we actually do walk or run, we always try to choose firm ground, which provides dependable and consistent support. The feeling of having stuck legs can also be experienced in the hypnopompic state, between sleeping and waking, when you become tangled up in your bed sheets and duvets.

56. NEGLECTED ANIMAL

Dream

You hear a whimpering sound from a box or a cupboard and when you open it, are saddened to find a terribly neglected animal inside. The animal is often a domestic pet, which has somehow been forgotten about. It is usually terribly thirsty and hungry, so you rush around, bringing it food and water to revive it. Although you are worried that it is going to die right in front of your eyes, you begin to get really angry as you try and work out who could neglect such a beautiful animal in this way.

Meaning

If you dream about finding a neglected animal, there is some instinctive part of your nature that you have been unconsciously ignoring in your waking life. Finding the animal in a box or a cupboard suggests you have been trying to conceal your natural instincts for some reason. This is often due to a situation in daily life where it seems that you need to hide your real feelings in order to peacefully coexist with other people. The neglected animal is usually a domestic pet and this can indicate that you have been neglecting your need for unconditional love and affection. It can often make you angry if you feel that the people closest to you are starving you of affection.

The type of animal you find reflects the kind of emotion that you feel is being neglected. Dogs and puppies represent your feelings of loyalty and affection, so a neglected dog can indicate that you feel someone close to you is being disloyal. Cats and kittens show your need for some independence and rabbits are your potential for healthy growth. Fish are your need to fully immerse yourself in your feelings now and again. Larger working animals, such as horses, symbolize your ability to harness your unconscious energy and put it to work for you. As well as reflecting your need for love and affection, the neglected animal can also suggest that you have been ignoring your more playful animal side.

Action

This dream is calling your attention to the areas of your life where you may be neglecting your needs. You have probably been spending much of your time looking after the needs of others, rather than attending to what you really need for yourself. You might have hoped others would recognize the

care and attention you give them but they might seem to be just taking you for granted. Animals are unable to voice their deeper instincts and needs but you can give voice to your concerns by speaking up and saying what you really need.

Background

After our parents, one of the first things we learn to show affection for is usually a soft cuddly animal toy, such as a teddy bear. This animal becomes the object of our unconditional affections and we often feel unequivocal love is reflected back to us from the toy. As we grow older, we may have a pet animal, which we care for in the same unconditional way, and we expect it to love us unconditionally, too. These cuddly toys and pets have come to represent our instinctual human need to love one another and be loved.

57. PURSUED BY ZOMBIES

Dream

You are in a public place in broad daylight and are horrified to find yourself being pursued by a gang of zombies. They move in such a ponderous way and you can't work out how they are gaining on you because you are running as fast as you possibly can. You try to avoid them but nothing stops their inevitable progress as they plod slowly towards you and they seem intent on turning you into one of the undead like them. Although zombies are the most common pursuers, you may also find yourself being chased by vampires or werewolves.

Meaning

Dreaming of being pursued by zombies suggests that you are involved in some dull repetitive activity in your waking life where you feel like you are just going through the motions. This activity is often associated with your professional life and usually involves mind-numbing tasks that seem to drain all the life energy from you. Being in this situation leaves you with very little time to pursue the hopes and ambitions that really matter to you. This can lead to you abandoning your most precious plans, particularly if you feel under pressure from peers or parents to do so. Although you thought your aspirations had been laid to rest, they have been lurking in limbo, waiting for an opportunity for you to bring them back to life..

The ponderous progress of the zombies reflects that you feel that you are getting nowhere in your professional life, even though you seem to be working as hard as you possibly can. Your fear of being caught suggests that you are afraid of becoming trapped in your current job and it will become a completely soul-destroying experience for you. The zombies have the potential to embody all the things you want to achieve, however, and are just waiting for you to breathe life back into them. Being pursued by vampires suggests that all your energy is being drained by an unhealthy romantic relationship. Pursuit by werewolves indicates that family commitments are allowing you no time to pursue your ambitions.

Action

This dream is alerting you to the fact that you have a unique talent that you have been ignoring. Although you assumed your opportunity to express this talent was dead and buried, it is time to breathe some new life into your efforts. By bringing

your ideas and plans back to life, you will revitalize your ambitions and feel like you have real purpose in your life again. Zombies usually try to eat the brains of their victims and this dream is urging you to use your brain to release yourself from conformity and really express your individuality.

Background

Even though zombies can seem quite monstrous, our key fear isn't that they will kill us, but that we will end up in a lethargic and lifeless limbo like them. Although zombies have become part of our popular culture through films such as George A Romero's 1968 film *Night of the Living Dead*, they were inspired by the Voodoo tradition of reanimated corpses being controlled by a sorcerer. This has come to symbolize how armies of workers have given up their individuality to be controlled by the bosses of a corporate machine, as powerfully depicted in Fritz Lang's 1926 film *Metropolis*.

58. UNFAMILIAR CITY OR STREET

Dream

You find yourself in the middle of an unfamiliar city or street. The buildings, the roads and the skyline all appear to be vaguely familiar but it looks as if their locations have been moved around in some way. It may seem as if the daylight or streetlights are strange, often seeming unusually intense or bright. You might try to orient yourself by looking for a street name you know or a road sign that can help you. Rather than just standing still, you choose a direction to go in and begin moving, hoping to find a familiar landmark.

Meaning

When you dream about a city, you are thinking about broader aspects of your life and the experience and wisdom you have accumulated so far in your lifetime. The city represents your wider public identity and the buildings are all the relationships you have built with other people over the years. The streets symbolize how these people are all connected and the skyline may indicate the people who figure most prominently from your current perspective. Although the layout of the city seems vaguely familiar, the fact that the street and building locations have moved into different places suggests you are considering the knowledge that you have built up and are looking at it in a variety of different ways.

The strange lighting you experience implies that you are looking at your accumulated experience and knowledge in a new light, and are reflecting on how you can constructively use it to illuminate new possibilities. As you try to orient yourself, you are familiarizing yourself with ways of exploring these opportunities, and looking at the road signs usually indicates you are searching for signals that confirm your intentions. Even though a city can seem familiar and unchanging, it is always moving and bustling with activity. This reflects the fact that you may feel quite happy and have no wish to change but one part of you is always out there, questing and looking, and wondering about new opportunities to make your mark.

Action

Although you may be feeling content with the familiar structure of your waking life, the message from this dream is that part of

you is always exploring, wondering about new possibilities to connect with something beyond yourself. This doesn't mean you have to change your life in any way, but that you are just opening yourself up to expanding your accumulations of knowledge, wisdom and experience. As you explore different ways of sharing your awareness, you will find yourself expanding the horizons of other people and becoming a familiar reference point for their explorations.

Background

Our cities are wonderful creations that have built up over a period of time, and in a similar way to our experience and wisdom, they provide us with an abundance of resources that are full of connections and possibilities. Like our knowledge and awareness, our cities may seem to be quite static but they are constantly changing and evolving. This continual reconstruction and re-imagining is shown in how we describe a city structure as a *'building'*, rather than a *'builded'* or a *'built'*. In the same way, we are continually evolving and always building on our accumulated experience and wisdom.

59. GETTING MARRIED OR DIVORCED

Dream

After what seems like a huge effort of planning and organization, you are walking down the aisle, on your way to get married. Although it is often a big ceremony, you might have the feeling that you are being pressured into the marriage. You may wonder about the commitment you are about to make and if you can really honour your vows. Sometimes you aren't quite sure whom you are marrying but you know that you need to get married. Even though you are happily married in waking life you can sometimes dream of becoming divorced or having been divorced.

Meaning

When you dream about getting married or divorced, you are considering a major decision or commitment in your waking life. Marriage symbolizes the successful union of two opposites and this dream suggests that you are trying to marry two quite different aspects of your life together. It may be that you want to start a family and are thinking about how you can balance this with your work obligations. It might also reflect that you have taken on an additional commitment in your current job and are deciding how to integrate it with what you do already. Although you know that this arrangement should work in theory, you realize you will have to walk a fine line in order to make it work in practice.

If you are feeling pushed or pressured into marriage then it usually indicates that you are putting yourself under a lot of pressure to accommodate these new commitments. Even though you are privately anxious about the impending workload, you put on a brave face and assure everyone that you can cope with it. Not knowing the identity of the bride or groom suggests you are unsure what you are really committing yourself to, and that you doubt that you will have much time for yourself if you take on these commitments. Dreaming of a divorce suggests that you feel you are committing too much time and effort into a particular obligation in waking life and you want to stop because it is really throwing your life off balance.

Action

The message from this dream is that you are trying to balance your commitments and honour the promises you have made to other people. It can be difficult to service all these obligations and it can become very easy for you to start to feel out of balance. Rather than becoming overly concerned about your commitments to others, spend some time thinking about your obligations to yourself. The more you can balance your needs and ambitions, the easier it will be for you to acknowledge the compromises you might need to make with other people.

Background

One of the biggest decisions a person can make in their life is to commit to a lifelong partnership with their significant other, and so getting married has come to symbolize making a deep and long-term commitment. Marriage is a blessing, and a source of great strength and comfort, but it also can be an area of compromise where we try and balance our needs with the needs of another in a mutual loving partnership. This conjugal relationship becomes a mutually powerful merging of needs and interests, but when these can no longer be met, it can end in divorce.

60. DARK BASEMENT

Dream

You hear a strange noise coming from your basement and, although you try to ignore it, you feel that you should investigate. As you open the door to the basement, you may be really scared because you have no idea what might be lurking down there in the dank and mouldy corners. You make your way fearfully down the stairs with your torch casting scary shadows on the damp walls. The basement may be flooded and you are sure something terrible is going to spring out at you but you are surprised when you find out what is actually making the noise.

Meaning

If you dream about something happening in the basement, it often shows that you are becoming aware of your fundamental behaviours and how they show up in waking life. Your house symbolizes your self and the basement represents your basic behaviours and how these provide a foundation for how you instinctively behave. Although you may try and ignore your baser instincts, this dream shows that some situation is bringing them into your conscious awareness. You may be anxious about exploring them in more depth because you feel you have no idea what might be lurking in the unknown areas of your character. As you try to illuminate these characteristics, they can often seem much darker and scarier than they actually are.

The basement is often flooded because water symbolizes your emotions and these foundational instincts are usually driven by how you feel rather than by rational thought processes. The mould and fungi show there is great potential for growth in your fundamental behaviours but you really need to start shining some light on them. Your biggest fear may be that your instincts and impulses will rise up and get the better of you, causing unwelcome disruption and conflict. But the

more you illuminate your underlying behaviours, the stronger and more secure your unique character will become. It can be tempting to try and hide these parts of yourself because you are unsure about them but they are fundamental parts of who you are.

Action

This dream is drawing your attention to the possibilities of looking more deeply inside yourself. It can sometimes feel unsettling to examine your deeper motivations but a healthy understanding of these basic urges is often the most reliable platform for achieving your deepest hopes and aspirations. The more you understand your fundamental behaviour patterns, the more solid and secure your personal foundations will be. Even though exploring your past experiences can seem dark and messy, they often hold vital information and resources that will make you feel far more grounded in your daily life.

Background

The house represents the self and the basement has come to represent the infrequently visited part of the psyche that actually supports the rest of the self. Although it can seem easier to keep a lid on them, the basement symbolizes a psychological storage space for foundational experiences, often giving rise to children's stories of monsters lurking in the cellar. It is often the utility space for plumbing and heating and so seems to emit all sorts of strange noises, only being entered if there is something untoward that can't be remedied elsewhere in the house.

61. CAUGHT UP IN A WAR

Dream

You are caught up in the middle of a major armed conflict, trying to escape the death and destruction by making your way to a safe place. Huge explosions are bursting all around, bullets are whizzing past and there is a constant feeling of danger. Although you are trying to avoid the conflict, you aren't actually fighting, and may find yourself stuck in a defensive position or rearguard action, trying to protect it against an adversary as you try to escape. You may also be trying to lead a group of people to a place of safety.

Meaning

Dreaming about being caught up in a war suggests you are experiencing some form of ongoing tension in your waking life. Although this may not be an open conflict with other people, the battle rumbles on endlessly inside you and whatever you do, you feel you can't reach the sanctuary of a peaceful compromise. Having conflicting needs, which you are finding it difficult to resolve, can often cause your tension. This may happen when you are forcing yourself to do something that you really don't want to do in order to try and keep the peace with someone. You feel that opening up and saying what you really think might be extremely destructive and would result in the end of your relationship with them.

Even though you try and keep your internal conflict under tight control, it can keep bursting out unexpectedly and causing

unintended damage. You have to watch what you say in case it causes an argument and you are constantly anxious about upsetting the other person. Although you are trying to resolve the situation amicably, you may find yourself having to be very defensive and this can appear quite hostile to the person you are dealing with. As well as trying to resolve your inner tensions, you may be attempting to resolve the conflicting needs of a larger group of people. This can make you an unwilling target for a lot of anger as people try and take their individual frustrations and tensions out on you.

Action

The message from this dream is that you are trying to avoid conflict and this is causing a lot of inner tension for you. The more you try to escape and evade this conflict, however, the more likely you are to be overpowered and drawn right into it. Rather than trying to run away from the situation, your best strategy is to bring your inner conflict out in the open and honestly confront it. Although this might make you feel vulnerable, it also places you fully in command of the battle and enables you to resolve it safely.

Background

While many of us don't have firsthand experience of being caught up in a war, our media is often filled with images of conflict. Many of our films and stories often take place against a background of war and some of the best known of these are about escape and evasion, such as John Sturges' 1963 film *The Great Escape*. Our language is full of phrases based on armed conflict, such as *'holding entrenched opinions'* and *'continually fortifying your position'*. We also talk about *'firing off an email'* or *'not sticking our heads above the parapet'*.

62. HOUSE BURGLARY

Dream

You are relaxing alone at home, often upstairs in bed, when you hear an unusual noise from outside the house. At first you are anxious that an intruder may be trying to break in but you reassure yourself that everything is all right. Next you hear the sound of movement from another room and you realize that a burglar has broken into your house. Although you want to stop them, you don't want to confront them in case they physically harm you in some way. Your main concern is that they will steal all your valuable possessions and wreck your house.

Meaning

If you dream that your house is being burgled, you feel that something unwelcome is intruding on your personal boundaries in waking life. A house usually represents your self in your dreams and is the place where you feel most secure and at home with yourself. Your bed symbolizes your private space where you can relax in comfort. The unusual sound outside indicates something is changing in your daily life and this is threatening your feelings of security in some way. This change may seem to be a really positive opportunity but it also may involve some elements that you feel are personally intrusive. Although you try to reassure yourself that everything is all right, the situation is starting to make you feel a bit uncomfortable.

The realization that the burglar has actually broken in shows your feelings of helplessness to prevent this intrusion into your private

space. Although you would like to confront the person crossing your personal boundaries in waking life, you also feel it might be harmful to your pursuit of the opportunities that they are offering to you. Your valuable possessions represent the personal qualities that you value most in yourself and so you feel that this intrusion is diminishing your sense of self-worth in some way. No matter how exciting the opportunity seems, you need to maintain your personal boundaries and not just give your valuable self away.

Action

This dream is alerting you to a situation where you are feeling insecure about allowing someone to enter your private life. Although you are normally quite open and welcoming, you are concerned that this person isn't recognizing your real worth and they may be taking you for granted in some way. Rather than allowing other people to take advantage of your valuable skills and hard-earned experience, you need to establish some personal boundaries to make them aware of your true value to them. The firmer you are in claiming your self-worth, the more secure you will feel.

Background

In the same way that our houses contain valued possessions, they also contain valued private and personal space. Very often the shock of a burglary isn't just that prized possessions have been stolen, but also that our private space has been invaded. Although we are happy to welcome others into our personal space, we do not enjoy it if they do so without permission and instead of being a welcoming pleasure it becomes an unwarranted intrusion. Usually, we don't feel that we will be harmed when someone intrudes on our space socially but it does prevent us from relaxing and being our real selves.

63. WRONG PAPERWORK

Dream

You are handing over your documents to an official and are dismayed when you are told that your paperwork is wrong. It may be that you are presenting your passport to a border guard or showing your ticket as you board a train. You were sure that your documents were valid but the official won't let you proceed with them. Your documentation might also be incomplete or have someone else's details on it. The official will often ask for your signature to prove your identity but you find that you can't sign your name, no matter how hard you try.

Meaning

When you dream of having the wrong paperwork, you are trying to assert your true identity in waking life and have it recognized and validated by other people. You may be having difficulty, however, in expressing who you really feel you are and this can be confusing for you and other people. Who you really are is most accurately reflected by your deeds and so your true identity is always mirrored in your actions and the choices you make. Although you would like to take these actions and make these choices without restrictions, you may often feel unqualified to do so and find yourself looking to others to validate your intentions and decisions.

You may be comfortable making choices and taking these actions in familiar territory but the border represents an unfamiliar boundary that you want to go beyond. Your passport

symbolizes your official and validated identity, while travel tickets represent your authority to proceed with a particular decision. Seeing someone else's details on the paperwork may indicate that you feel like a bit of an impostor or are looking to someone else to give you the go-ahead. Hands are how you create and shape your future so a wobbly hand indicates that you are finding it difficult to decide what to do and put it into action. Even though you know that you have the abilities to take the next step, you feel that you need official sanction to do so.

Action

The message from this dream is that you are trying to validate your unique identity, while spending most of your time looking to other people in the hope they will recognize your uniqueness and permit you to be yourself. Rather than waiting for others to give you permission to be who you really want to be, it is time to claim your identity by breaking down your self-imposed barriers. Although it may be comforting to be officially recognized by others, you have the ultimate authority in deciding who you are and who you really want to be.

Background

In our dealings with the authorities, proving our identity is one of the fundamental processes we undertake and until our identity is proven with an official document, we could be anyone. One of the key signifiers of our identity is our signature, and as children one of the first things that we learn to read and write are our names. Although the documents we carry may help to verify our physical identities, they do not describe the boundless opportunities we have to realize our true purpose and potential in life.

The Top 100 Dreams

64. DEEP IN A FOREST OR JUNGLE

Dream

You are making your way through a deep dense forest or jungle trying to get through to a more open area on the other side. There is a path you are following but it seems to be getting narrower and fainter. Branches brush against your face and the undergrowth tugs at your clothing. The trees are really tall and some have fallen down, their trunks blocking your way. You hear mysterious rustlings coming from all around you and there seem to be dark shapes moving in the shadows. Although it is scary, you keep pushing deeper and deeper.

Meaning

When you dream of being deep in a forest or jungle, you are becoming aware of unfamiliar parts of your character and their potential for growth in waking life. A forest symbolizes all your unconscious and unseen aspects that grow and mature over the years. Although you have not consciously been aware of these areas, a situation in waking life has compelled you to enter and explore them in more depth. This is often triggered when you revisit events from the past and are investigating how they may have affected you. Making your way through this deep dark forest to a clearing shows that you are trying to clear up some confusion about these events.

Although you think you had a definite issue to resolve when you began this self-exploration, it often becomes less and less defined as you explore further. The branches against your face

and the undergrowth tugging at your clothing indicate that you may be having your attention drawn to your identity and who you really think you are. As you progress on your journey, you encounter habitual barriers and blockages, which you have to confront or make your way around. The rustling and the shapes are your instinctive impulses, which you fear may harm you in some way. Even though it is frightening, you get more confident the deeper you go and you finally start to realize what is at the root of the situation.

Action

The main insight from this dream is that you have access to a rich and varied collection of resources within your self. Although these areas may appear mysterious and uncontrollable they contain valuable information about your growth as a person. As you continue on your journey of self-exploration, it is important not to lose sight of where you have come from and where you want to go. Choose the path you want to follow and try not to be distracted by all the other routes that you are being advised to take.

Background

Our first encounters with mysterious forests are usually from children's stories about enchanted woods. The fairy-tale forests often hold something of great value but it usually takes courage and persistence to find it and return with the prize. Forests and jungles are also sanctuaries for mysterious and powerful characters like Robin Hood or indigenous Amazonian tribes. Somewhere within all our inner landscapes is a wild wood where we can truly be ourselves. Like our dream forests, our unknown and unseen places are often a sanctuary where we can rest and recover in our waking lives.

65. MYSTERIOUS CORRIDOR

Dream

You open a door while exploring a building and find a mysterious corridor stretching out in front of you. The corridor is long, sometimes curving off into the distance and has lots of doors leading off from it. It may be bright and well lit or appear like a dark and shadowy passage. You feel quite cautious about venturing down the passageway because you aren't sure what you might encounter further down there. As you start moving along it, you pluck up courage to try a few of the door handles and peep into the rooms. You are often surprised with what you find inside.

Meaning

When you dream about a mysterious corridor, you are often reflecting on opportunities for change in your waking life. A building symbolizes your self and doorways usually represent the thresholds that you have to cross in order to step into new opportunities. The door you open symbolizes a boundary you are negotiating in your waking life and this has started you on a path that makes a number of other opportunities available to you. These possible courses of action are stretching out in front of you and some of them may appear brighter and clearer than others. If there are just a few doors then you probably have just a few options to choose from. Lots of doors suggest you feel overwhelmed by choices.

The corridor can also feel like a maze where you open one door and it leads to another corridor, which leads into another, until you feel completely lost and disoriented. This can indicate that you feel forced into making decisions that are taking you further and further from where you want to be. Venturing down the passageway also represents a rite of passage where you have to leave the past behind in order to step fully into your future. Working your way along this passage is often a process of discovering unrealized possibilities, however, rather than encountering unpleasant surprises. The corridor usually leads into a much greater appreciation of your self and all the talents and resources that you possess.

Action

The thread running through this dream is that you are travelling through a period of change and need to make some choices about what is best for you. Although you may feel you are being forced to follow a particular path, you have the power to open up a whole lot of possibilities. You may feel anxious about crossing this threshold but it will allow you to step into a new area of your life. The best way to make your choice is to take some time to explore each of the opportunities opening up for you.

Background

The rooms in a building symbolize different aspects of your character and the corridors are how you transition between these aspects of yourself and discover previously unknown opportunities in the process. All cultures have rites of passage where participants take part in a ritual that celebrates their transition from one significant stage of their life into another. This process of self-discovery is an instinctive and dynamic

progression. The word *'corridor'* is derived from the Italian *correre*, meaning *'to run'* and reflects this natural movement and flow from one life-stage to another.

66. BEING PREGNANT

Dream

Your abdomen has become huge and swollen, and you realize you are pregnant and about to give birth. Although your baby bump appears to have grown unusually quickly, it seems to be taking a while for your newborn to actually emerge. The bump also seems to be getting in the way of your day-to-day living and is becoming quite awkward to manoeuvre as you walk around. When you do give birth, it may be to unusual creatures and objects or often a really ugly baby. You may also dream of having a miscarriage or terminating the pregnancy.

Meaning

If you dream that you are pregnant, it usually reflects a protracted period of waiting in the completion of a project or plan in your waking life. This gestation period suggests you have been developing a plan, which is about to be born into practical reality, and the dream is showing you the need to be patient and to provide adequate resources for the successful birth of the project. Although you may have conceived your plan quite recently, the realities of bringing it to life may be taking some time to put into practice. The extra weight of responsibility associated with the project may make it difficult to continue with your previous lifestyle and you may find that it limits your freedom to enjoy other activities.

When you do eventually bring your labour of love out into the world, you may dismayed that it doesn't live up to your expectations of what you hoped would emerge. If it seems a bit ugly or looks unusual, then there is some more work to be done in developing and nurturing your idea. Even though you may be a bit disappointed, you have still created something vigorous and healthy, which will grow into something beautiful over time. Dreaming of having a miscarriage or a termination can show that you feel a project may have to be aborted because of outside influences beyond your control. Like most worthwhile experiences, there is often some time between planting the seed and seeing that potential come to life.

Action

The message from this dream is that you are about to create something wonderful but you need to take it easy and just allow things to progress at a natural pace. The key action isn't to focus on the outcome but to look after yourself in preparation for this great opportunity that is about to appear. You have to be patient and wait for the natural process to take its course so it can develop over the fullness of time. This can be quite a laborious experience but it gives your budding ambitions the best possible chance of success.

Background

Being pregnant is one of the most powerful human conditions and it demonstrates our continuing ability to create something new by using our available resources and creativity. All cultures have fertility rites and their associated symbols, such as Easter

eggs or Egyptian frogs. Much of our language about ideas and planning is derived from words and phrases associated with pregnancy and fertility. We speak of *'conceiving a plan'*, *'working on a conceptual idea'* and *'having a fertile imagination'*. We also associate pregnancy with a feeling of expectancy, such as when we use the phrase a *'pregnant pause'*.

67. POTENTIALLY FATAL INJURY

Dream

You are engaged in some seemingly harmless and routine activity when you suddenly find yourself being attacked. Your assailant appears from nowhere and strikes a potentially fatal blow before you even have a chance to register what is going on. The weapon is usually something that just comes to hand such as a kitchen knife or hammer, with the attacker giving you no warning of their murderous intentions. Even though your injuries could prove fatal, you are more concerned with the motive for the attack and why you, an apparently innocent victim, have been singled out.

Meaning

If you dream you have sustained a potentially fatal injury, then you are probably experiencing a situation in your waking life where you feel terribly wounded emotionally. This emotional wounding usually occurs because of a sudden severing of a close partnership or romantic relationship. Your assailant seems to appear from nowhere because you just didn't see this coming and it has taken you completely by surprise. Although you felt that everything was healthy in your relationship, it now feels as if your life has been ripped apart. The weapon used by your attacker is often an everyday object because the discord was apparently triggered by a minor disagreement, perhaps over some routine domestic event or work situation.

Your main concern is usually not the severity of your injuries, but why you were actually attacked in the first place. Although you may feel that you are the innocent victim of an unprovoked assault, it may be that you have been quite complacent in the relationship and haven't picked up on a number of signs that forewarned of increasing unease. These warning signals may have been quite subtle but being more aware would have enabled you to tackle the situation in a more effective manner. Being singled out reflects your anxieties about being left alone by this split in your relationship or partnership. If you experience death in a dream, it usually signifies a fundamental transformation, and your potentially fatal injuries suggest that you have to transform your life by just moving on.

Action

The message from this dream is that you may be leaving yourself open to disappointment by becoming too complacent about a particular relationship or partnership. It can be tempting to become paranoid and suspicious about your partner's intentions but this can make you feel like even more of a victim as you constantly check up on them. Instead of assuming that your partner will always be there for you, try connecting with them more honestly and intentionally. The more respectful you are of the bond between you, the less likely it is to be suddenly broken.

Background

It is very fortunate in our modern age that the threat of a potentially fatal injury is extremely remote, but many of the words and phrases that we use when talking about separation still use quite violent imagery. When we talk about financial dealings, we speak of funding being subject to *'savage cuts'*, having to part with a large sum of money as *'costing an arm and a leg'* or a particular public service *'being axed'*. In emotional trauma, we say that we are *'feeling really cut up about it'* or it being a real *'slap in the face'*.

68. ANIMAL IN THE GARDEN

Dream

You are relaxing in your garden when you hear a rustling from the undergrowth. Branches are shaking and leaves are twitching and you realize that there is some type of wild animal out there. Although you can't see the animal clearly, you feel it might harm you, so you try to get back to the house as quickly as you can. As you rush towards the door, the animal breaks cover and bounds after you. Even though you get back inside the house, the animal may get a paw through the door or bang against a window.

Meaning

When you dream about an animal in your garden you are usually reflecting on how you control your instinctive impulses in social

situations. Your house symbolizes your self and as the garden is the area just beyond your immediate self, it often represents close friends and relationships you have cultivated. Like your friendships, the plants in the garden often grow naturally and blossom with their own rhythms. The undergrowth around the plants represents the unknown and unspoken areas in your relationships. These untamed parts of the garden show potential areas of growth in your connections with others. This dream indicates that you are picking up signs and clues that are making you wonder about your behaviour in your relationships.

The wild animal represents the instinctive and impulsive part of yourself, which you try and contain in social settings with other people. The threat is that something in your immediate social environment will trigger instinctual impulses and cause you to act out of character and lose control. You are scared that if you can't contain these instincts they will somehow compromise the identity that you present to other people. Rather than being an intrusion, it is an opportunity to rediscover the power of your innate strength and wisdom. This animal in the garden often represents your confidence and your power to assert yourself. Although you would like to tame and housetrain your instincts, sometimes you have to freely acknowledge their wisdom and energy.

Action

This dream is revealing that you are concerned about reacting too impulsively in a social situation. This can result, however, in you acting quite unnaturally when you are out and about with your friends and companions. Although this may seem safer and more socially acceptable to others, it also means that they are missing out on the wonderful richness and complexity of the real you. By giving yourself some space to connect with your true nature, you often find that you really begin to flourish and your social life starts to bloom.

Background

When we are children, the garden is often the first area that we experience outside the house. It opens up our awareness and is full of unfamiliar sights and sounds and smells. Although the garden can be well cultivated and cared for, being closer to nature takes us closer to our natural instincts and impulses. The garden has a natural rhythm with flowers and crops following natural cycles. Even though we refer to something as *'common or garden'*, it usually describes part of our innate nature rather than something unremarkable.

69. ESCAPING FROM A TORNADO

Dream

Although this dream often starts off with you being in a safe and secure place, such as your home, you usually have a deep sense of foreboding that something disruptive is about to happen. As you look into the distance, the sky becomes darker and you see a destructive and powerful storm approaching, usually in the form of a whirling tornado. You may be able to escape but it seems inevitable that you will be caught up in the chaos. Instead of fleeing, you cling on to whatever solid objects you can, and hold on tight as the tornado wreaks havoc around you.

Meaning

When you dream about the weather, you are reflecting on all the eventualities and outcomes that you can't possibly control in your waking life. Like the weather, there are some aspects of your life that aren't under your control and this dream often occurs when there is something potentially disruptive looming on the horizon. In a dream, the sky symbolizes your thinking and so this impending disruption may be causing you to have some dark thoughts. The whirling tornado represents a mental turmoil that you don't want to be drawn into because you know that it might be quite upsetting for you. It can be very easy to get caught up in a whirl of negative thinking and find yourself being carried away by it all.

You may be able to step out of the path of the oncoming disruption by standing aside from the developing situation. If it seems inevitable that you will be caught up in all the turmoil, the best way to stay grounded during this commotion is to hold onto what is stable and secure in your daily life. Like the eye of the storm, you will often achieve clarity of thinking and vision when the disruption is at its most powerful and strongest. You can't contain these whirling thoughts, you can only shelter from them until the situation blows over. As the storm subsides you realize that you are a stronger person than you thought and a lot of unnecessary anxieties have been blown away.

Action

This dream is forecasting that a wind of change may be about to start blowing through your daily routine. Although you may not be able to prevent this transformation, you can use it to your advantage by making the most of the disruption. Rather than just waiting for the imminent chaos to arrive, make a plan to ensure that you can look after yourself and those who are close to you. It may be difficult to stay grounded but by sticking to what you know and trust you will find it easier to weather the storm and emerge unscathed after it has all blown over.

Background

We are often unaware of the air that envelops us all and the atmosphere can seem like a largely empty space, so it can come as a huge surprise when this apparent emptiness generates forces powerful enough to disrupt and destroy solid and stable structures. Tornadoes often form during volatile and oppressive weather conditions such as thunderstorms where the atmosphere fills with powerful air currents. This dramatic weather pattern has come to represent our inner turmoil, as disruptive events often seem to appear out of nowhere and threaten to wreak havoc with our daily routines.

70. MALFUNCTIONING MACHINE

Dream

A machine, which is usually reliable and consistent, begins to malfunction for no apparent reason. You might be trying to use it for a simple and routine task but it just won't cooperate in the way it should. Even though you repeatedly switch it off and on again, shout at it and bang it on the side, it still doesn't work. The machine may go completely out of control, becoming dangerous and threatening, making you think that it has become possessed with a life of its own and you can't do anything to control it.

Meaning

Dreaming about a malfunctioning machine often indicates that a normally predictable situation is starting to disintegrate in your waking life. This can occur when there is a communication breakdown between yourself and someone you regularly rely on. Although you may be used to dealing with their familiar and habitual behaviours, this can result in you taking them for granted because you always expect that they will behave in the same way. These assumptions can cause an accumulation of hidden stress and tension, which eventually leads to a failure in communication. No matter how frequently and loudly you try and get your message across, the other person just won't cooperate in the way that you would like them to.

Rather than adjusting your behaviour, you keep trying to adjust the other person so that they will continue to behave in the way that you have come to expect them to. It may seem as if the other person has become irrational and they are threatening your relationship. The key to restoring a healthy relationship is to stop treating yourself and other people as machines. It can be easy to think of other people as automatons, having predictable responses to specific inputs and with problems that can be easily fixed by some simple behavioural upgrade. Other people have lives of their own and although you can connect with and influence them, trying to control them will often result in a relationship breakdown.

Action

In this dream, you are being alerted to a potential failure in communication with someone who you tend to depend on. This can often happen in relationships, where everything seems to be normal, but there are unspoken tensions under the surface. These stresses may accumulate over time and cause a breakdown during periods of particular strain. Rather than trying to repair a relationship after the damage has been done, it is best to put regular effort into maintaining the quality of your connections with other people. This usually ensures that they will be there for you when you need them most.

Background

One of the key differences between humans and most other species is our ability to use tools. We become so accustomed to using our tools and machines that they often seem to become extensions of our actions and ourselves. We then extend this behaviour into anthropomorphism where we ascribe personalities to our machines, such as giving pet names to our cars and musical instruments. This is also reflected in how people sometimes express themselves using terminology that is more often used to describe machinery, such as *'blowing a gasket'* or being as *'regular as clockwork'*.

71. BECOMING A SUPERHERO

Dream

You are confronted with a terribly destructive situation and feel absolutely powerless to do anything about it. It may be an impending natural disaster, or perhaps the appearance of a monster or a supervillain. You are desperate to protect your loved ones from the approaching danger and are delighted to realize that you have superpowers, which you didn't know you

had. Soon you find yourself moving mountains and shooting X-ray beams from your eyes as you keep everyone safe by warding off death and destruction. After you have dealt with the danger, you revert back to your normal self.

Meaning

Dreams of becoming a superhero are often triggered when you feel trapped and powerless by a particular situation in waking life. This situation seems completely insurmountable but, because it has become part of your daily life, it also feels quite normal and routine. It may be that you have to deal with ongoing family tensions or a long-term health problem and it makes you think that you are stuck in an endless grind that you can never escape from. Although your situation seems hopeless, this dream confirms that you are actually dealing with it very effectively. Your superhero powers indicate that you have fantastic inner resources, which consistently enable you to rise above all the challenges you face in your apparently powerless and ordinary life.

These superpowers become apparent in all the choices you make and actions you take when dealing with your challenging circumstances. A key characteristic of most superheroes is they have an extremely well-developed moral sense of right and wrong. Even though you are constantly faced with arduous challenges, you never shirk away from them and always try and do the right thing for everyone involved in the situation. Rather than acting in your self-interest, doing the right thing gives you the ability to move mountains and see right into the heart of the matter. After you have finished dealing with the situation and ensured that everyone else is all right, you take some time to look after your needs.

Action

This dream is revealing that you are far more powerful than you realize or will admit to other people. You usually only step into your power, however, when you feel that someone that you love is in jeopardy. Even after you have taken care of your loved one and apparently slipped back into the normality of everyday life, you still have the ability to call on your resources and focus your power. Rather than just waiting for someone to come along and rescue you, you can use your powers to lift you up and take you where you want to go.

Background

Although we think of superpower stories as a comparatively modern phenomenon, starting with Siegel and Shuster's *Superman* comics in 1932, our ancestors also had characters that appeared to possess superhuman powers. One of the best-known superheroes in Greek mythology was the warrior Achilles, and, like today's more modern superheroes, his superpowers couldn't protect him from feeling vulnerable. In the same way that Superman has his kryptonite and Achilles had his heel, your ability to take care of other people can sometimes be impaired if you do not take time to look after your own needs.

72. STRANGER WITH A MESSAGE

Dream

You meet a stranger who tells you they have an important message for you. The stranger is very keen to give you the message but you are concerned because you have never met them before and are unsure of their intentions. You feel the message may be bad news or some sort of threatening letter or official warning. Even though the stranger seems to know a lot about you, they still ask you to identify yourself to ensure the right person is getting the message. Sometimes the stranger seems to have a completely forgettable face or no face at all.

Meaning

Dreaming of a stranger with a message reflects the fact that your intuitive awareness of a situation is often more insightful and instructive than your conscious and logical thought processes. Although you may feel you know yourself very well from a rational perspective, there is often a large part of your potential that is unexplored. This undiscovered area is often full of hidden talents and unrealized ambitions. It contains a natural wisdom that can be difficult to access because you are unfamiliar with the language this unknown part of yourself uses to express your gifts. The stranger you meet represents this part of yourself that you don't really know but is coming more and more into your conscious awareness.

The very important message the stranger has for you is invariably from yourself, usually from the unfamiliar part of yourself that your unconscious awareness is trying to draw to your attention. This dream is often triggered when you start to explore a new situation in waking life and you begin to realize talents that you didn't know you had. You may initially be unsure of your developing skills and may even find them quite threatening. The stranger knows a lot about you because they actually are you, and wants to make sure that you are fully aware of your potential. A forgettable or faceless stranger indicates that it is time to face up to your potential and to start using your dormant talents.

Action

The message from this dream is that you often actually know a lot more than you consciously realize. Your unconscious awareness is absorbing huge amounts of information from your surroundings constantly, but this is filtered out by your conscious awareness, and so you aren't usually aware of all the knowledge that you are receiving. By paying greater attention to all these unconscious clues, you can start to become much more aware of the potential opportunities to be realized in any situation you find yourself in. Although this may seem strange at first, you soon start to appreciate its real value.

Background

One of the most prevalent characters in folklore and legend is the mysterious stranger who arrives at a time of need and then disappears again. This stranger is often revealed to be a king or queen in disguise trying to find out the real story about a particular situation. These strangers often become mythologized, particularly in genres describing new areas of opportunity such as Westerns. The heroic figure in classic films like *Shane*, *High Plains Drifter* and *Pale Rider* is a mysterious stranger who personifies an important lesson to be learned.

73. LOST AT THE SHOPS

Dream

You have gone to the shops to buy something that you are sure you need, but are finding it really difficult to find the shop you want to go to. When you eventually do get to the shop, you are quite anxious that you don't have enough money to make your purchase. You look around for alternative things to buy instead but can't make up your mind what you actually need the most. The shop assistants are usually really unhelpful, trying to convince you to buy things that you don't genuinely need or seem far too expensive to you.

Meaning

When you dream of being lost at the shops, you are sometimes unsure of how to realize your true value in waking life. Shops are filled with items for sale, usually with their value clearly displayed on price tags, and your ability to buy these items is often determined by your personal worth. Trying to find the right shop suggests you are finding it difficult to find a situation in your daily life that will allow you to really demonstrate your real value. Although you may eventually find the shop, not having enough money shows that you may have found the right showcase for your abilities but lack the confidence to have your talents fully recognized by others.

If you lack self-assurance in your ability to do what you really want to, then you often shop around for opportunities where other people will more readily value your talents. Relying on others for your sense of worth, however, can make it difficult to decide where you are valued most. Banking on other people for your sense of value is reflected in the behaviour of the shop assistants. Their unhelpful attitude shows that others aren't helping you find your real value or are failing to recognize your true worth. The most valuable thing you can possess is a confident sense of self-worth as it can be difficult to fulfil your needs if you do not value yourself enough.

Action

The message from this dream is that you are more valuable than you think but you are finding it difficult to state your true worth in your relationships or in the workplace. This is because you aren't really valuing yourself enough and are just giving yourself away to others, with no recognition of your true value. One of the best ways to ensure that others do recognize your value is to just say *'No'* to them when you feel their demands are unreasonable. This will stop you being taken for granted and help you to claim your real worth.

Background

From the first time we buy sweets with our pocket money, shops are places where we demonstrate our worth and command the attention of others. This feeling continues into adulthood where we can continue to assert our self-worth by indulging in bouts of retail therapy. We are often addicted to bargain hunting and sales because they help us to realize that we are actually a lot more valuable than we usually think we are. Our word *'credit'* is derived from the Latin *credere*, meaning *'to believe'*, and the more we believe in ourselves, the more valuable we become.

74. MUTILATED OR MISSING BODY PART

Dream

You have suffered some sort of terrible injury to your body but are viewing this situation with a strange air of detachment. The

injury may be a dismemberment where some part of your body has burst open and your insides are spilling out. You may have lost a major part of your body, such as a leg or an arm, or your head may have been cut off. Even though you are horrifically injured in this gory situation, you try to carry on as if nothing had happened and are working out how you can continue to function with this debilitating injury.

Meaning

When you dream of suffering a major bodily injury, you feel that your usual ability to take action is somehow being impaired in your waking life. You use the different parts of your body image to represent different aspects of your purpose and potential. When these parts of your body are mutilated or missing in your dream, you are concerned that your ability to function in that area of your life is somehow being debilitated and compromised. If you have been dismembered and your insides seem to be spilling out, then you sense that you may be opening up too much to other people and are forgetting to look after your personal boundaries and needs.

Losing other body parts can show where you feel frustrated from reaching your potential. Your legs carry you forward through life and give you power to progress. Your feet are where you stand and what you value. Your arms are the ability to take action and assert yourself. Your hands are how you shape and control your future. Your head is how you think and contains your sense of logic and rationality. Your heart is how you feel and connect to other people close to you. Even though you have lost a seemingly vital part of yourself, you just work around it and try and carry on with what you are doing. Rather than ask for help, you may continue to conceal your frustrations.

Action

This dream is reconnecting you with your ability to take vital action. Although you may initially feel at a bit of a loss, you are making the most of the remaining resources you have. These surviving parts of your potential may take some time to develop again and the best way to reconnect with them is to start connecting with other people. Even though you would like to try and resolve this situation on your own, there are others who will be more than happy to lend you a hand until you find your feet again.

Background

Much of our language about taking action, or being frustrated from taking action, is based on body parts. We tend to view our bodies as machines made from discrete components rather than as organic wholes, and so we speak of our *'heart not being in it'*, *'not having the stomach for a fight'*, *'head ruling the heart'* and *'not having a leg to stand on'*. Although the vast majority of us will be fortunate enough not to sustain any bodily injuries during our lives, we often encounter graphically gory scenes in films, on television and in computer games.

75. TRAPPED IN A LIFT

Dream

You are travelling in a lift as you try to reach a specific floor in a tall building. You really need to get to this floor because you

have to attend an important appointment there. But when you reach your intended floor, the lift doors jam and you are trapped inside. You try pushing the buttons but none of them seem to work and even if you do get the lift moving, it never goes to the floor you want. Sometimes there is a sickening lurch and you are scared that the lift will plummet to the bottom of the shaft.

Meaning

When you dream of being trapped in a lift, it usually indicates that you are feeling frustrated about your upward progress in your particular profession; the lift symbolizes a specific way to advance from one recognized professional level to another. It often seems to be a logical progression with definite steps to take, buttons to press and choices to make. A tall building represents the potential for higher levels of achievement and an important appointment shows a chance to reach a particular level of fulfilment. The doors jamming show that the opportunity isn't opening up in the way you would like it to and becoming trapped in the lift shows that you are feeling stuck in your promotion prospects.

This can make you feel boxed in and as if you are getting nowhere. Pushing the buttons shows that you are trying to take some specific actions to continue your upward progress but none of these procedures seem to be having any effect. Arriving at the wrong floor indicates that even when you do get your career moving again, it doesn't take you to where you really want to go. You think you know what you want but when you arrive at your chosen level and step into your new future, it turns out to be a different story. If the lift lurches and is about to plummet, then you feel insecure in your progress and are anxious you might have to start all over again.

Action

This dream is indicating that you feel too constrained in your current choice of career path and are wondering how to move out beyond it. It can be easy to suffer from tunnel vision as you plan your promotional path within an organization. The key to releasing yourself from the lift is to start thinking outside the box about your possible career directions. Rather than just relying on successive promotions, you may like to put in some effort and see what other steps you might take. Try exploring work that really elevates your spirits rather than just your promotional prospects.

Background

We tend to associate professional success with the towering glass and steel skyscrapers of city business districts. Executives who have achieved a recognized level of status within their organizations usually occupy the upper floors of these pinnacles. The main method of travelling to these higher levels is by using the lift. It is possible to use the stairs but this is slow and requires enormous effort, so it is much easier to make use of the existing corporate machinery. But taking the easy option can blinker us to the world of possibilities that lie beyond the confines of the lift walls.

76. LEAKING ROOF

Dream

You notice that water is coming into your house and realize the roof is leaking. The leak starts off as a small drip through

the ceiling but then grows into a trickle and then a flood. Water continues to run down the inside walls and you become concerned about the flood damage that the water might cause. Although a huge volume of water is pouring into the house, you often can't see where the leak is actually coming from. You are concerned that the water will wash away the walls causing your house to collapse and leaving you with nowhere to live.

Meaning

When you dream about a leaking roof, you are often trying to resolve some form of emotional insecurity in your waking life. The different parts of a house usually represent the different aspects of your character and the roof symbolizes your need for shelter and overall security. The roof is at the top of the house and also indicates how you contemplate your thoughts and ideas. Water symbolizes your emotions and feelings, so a leaking roof symbolizes some emotionally fraught situation, which is making you feel quite irrational and insecure. Although you are trying to think logically through this situation and work out the best course of action, you sometimes can't help your emotions running away with you.

The water usually starts off as an annoying trickle as you become aware of these emotions seeping into your analytical thought processes. But the more that you try to deal with your emotions in a rational manner, the more your feelings will build up into a flood. The walls of your house symbolize your personal boundaries and trying to suppress your feelings will cause your emotional barriers to become even more fragile. Your concern at the water washing away the walls indicates you are anxious about breaking down emotionally as you might lose your sense of self and your ability to support your choices. Even though the sheer volume of water seems unbelievable, it reflects the power of your feelings in this situation.

Action

This dream is opening you up to working through your feelings instead of just trying to analyse them logically. It can be easy to dismiss your emotions, but they can often provide a more accurate indication of your circumstances than a rational analysis. In this situation, your feelings are encouraging you to establish clear boundaries with other people to ensure that you don't neglect your needs. The best way to do this is by just expressing how you really feel when you are being swamped by the demands of others.

Background

As well as being used to describe the flow of water through a seemingly impermeable barrier, we also use the word *'leak'* to characterize information that has been communicated outside normal channels. These leaks often expose people who thought that they were in a secure and comfortable position and they often spend a great deal of effort plugging the flow of information after they have been compromised. Even though we feel we have nothing to hide, we can feel uncomfortably exposed if our emotions start leaking out, no matter how much we try to control them.

77. THREATENED BY A SPIDER

Dream

You are relaxing when you become aware of a huge spider about to drop on you. Even though you aren't frightened of spiders in waking life, you can see it really clearly above your head and it is truly terrifying. You may also find yourself entangled in an endless sticky web and the more you struggle, the more enmeshed you become. The spider may also have poison dripping from its fangs and you are scared that you will be bitten. Depending on the situation, you may also find yourself being threatened by a giant octopus or sea serpents.

Meaning

Dreaming of being threatened by a spider suggests that you are anxious about being emotionally entangled in a particular situation in waking life. Becoming emotionally enmeshed is a threat to your happiness and wellbeing because you are concerned that somehow you will end up trapped in a complex situation and be unable to move. This emotional complexity often involves a family situation or perhaps a romantic one. Even though you are committed to the relationship, you are anxious it will start to devour all your time and energy and become a sticky situation from which there isn't any escape. Although the trap may be very strong, much of it will be subtle, slowly building up over time and woven together from many different threads.

Being afraid of being bitten by a venomous spider indicates that you don't want to be drawn into a poisonous war of words with someone you have a relationship with, as you are scared it will be a painful experience and leave you unable to take any further action to resolve the situation. Dreams of being attacked by sea creatures are more common in romantic relationships. Grasping octopus tentacles and entwining sea serpents symbolize strong feelings rising from your emotional depths, which threaten to overwhelm you. This suggests you are unconsciously concerned about becoming more involved in a relationship because you fear powerful feelings of jealousy will rise to the surface and potentially transform you into a green-eyed monster.

Action

This dream is encouraging you to disentangle yourself from a situation where you feel emotionally trapped. It might feel as if it is difficult to extricate yourself from this position because there are a number of connections that seem to be holding you back. Although you have the power to break free, you are worried that your actions will let a number of people down. The best way to disengage yourself is to view your situation in a more detached manner and to really say how you feel. The more honestly you can express your feelings, the more freedom everyone will gain.

Background

Although most spiders are small inoffensive creatures, many of us have an irrational fear of them. Humans have always imbued spiders with special qualities, from the Greek myths of Athena and Arachne to the present day adventures of Spider-Man. Many of these stories involve tales of guilt and betrayal within

families and we still use phrases like *'being drawn into a web of deceit'* or *'being spun a line'*. In the same way that a spider spins its web, involvement in these emotional entanglements usually builds up over a period of time, with no obvious attacks or aggression.

78. BAD FOOD

Dream

You are feeling hungry and looking for something to eat but even though you know what you would like, you are having difficulty in finding it, no matter how much you search. You might find yourself having a meal with someone but the food isn't healthy or filling. Although you may manage to find a restaurant, there is something wrong with the food on your plate, even though everyone else seems to be having normal healthy food. It just doesn't seem very appetizing or fresh and you would rather go hungry than put it in your mouth.

Meaning

If you dream of bad food then there is some situation in your waking life leaving you feeling badly unfulfilled and dissatisfied. Food represents your ability to fulfil yourself by satisfying your needs and gives you the energy to explore opportunities and make the most of them. Although you think you know what would make you more satisfied in life, it seems very difficult to find what you really need. Dreaming of having a meal with someone suggests that you are considering how fulfilling you find your relationship with him or her. Even though they seem to be satisfying some of your needs, you feel that there is something fundamentally unhealthy about the relationship and it leaves you feeling strangely empty and discontented.

A restaurant usually symbolizes how satisfied you feel about the work you do, and if there is something wrong with your food, then you are often feeling unfulfilled in your job. Even though all the other people working around you seem to enjoy their work, it may feel as if you have lost your appetite for yours. It might seem as if there are no fresh challenges in your current situation and that you are just processing the same old stuff again and again. If you are hungry for fulfilment and success, you need to move on and find a way of filling your life with rich and varied experiences that are more to your taste. By nourishing your ambitions, you will often realize more sustained satisfaction.

Action

This dream is suggesting that you are experiencing a situation that isn't nearly as fulfilling as you hoped it might be. Even though you have spent a lot of effort preparing for this opportunity, it hasn't turned out the way you thought it would. This can often happen when you spend all your time trying to look after the needs of others and can lead to quite unhealthy relationships. The more you can nurture your fundamental needs, the more you will be able to enjoy the satisfaction of looking after other people.

Background

Much of our language around being fulfilled is based on food. We speak about a need for fulfilment as having *'an appetite*

for success' and a potentially unwelcome outcome as a *'recipe for disaster'*. Foods that are enjoyable and easy to eat reflect a sense of almost effortless fulfilment and we hear this as being *'a piece of cake'* or *'easy as pie'*. More difficult situations, which are harder to cope with, are *'hard cheese'* or plans that are *'half-baked'*. If you are trying to fulfil a number of goals simultaneously, then you may have *'too much on your plate'*.

79. OLDEN TIMES

Dream

You find that you have travelled back in time to a period in history that seems to be centuries ago. Everyone is dressed in old-fashioned clothes, reminiscent of a period drama or historical reconstruction. They are engaged in activities that seem quite antiquated and labour-intensive but there is a certainty about their purpose. The people may be travelling on foot or in horse-drawn vehicles, and their accessories might look like museum exhibits. There is no sign of contemporary technology or any of the social infrastructure we usually take for granted in the modern world.

Meaning

When you dream about travelling back in time, it often indicates that you are thinking about your experiences of past events and considering how they may have influenced what is happening presently in your waking life. Although it might seem like centuries ago, your past contains many valuable experiences and forms the foundations of your current activities. The people in the dream symbolize aspects of your character that you feel you have left behind as you have progressed through life. Their old-fashioned clothes represent how you used to be and how you responded to the challenges you faced. The historical feel indicates that you are trying to piece together how your previous actions have brought you to your present position.

The fact that their activities seem quite antiquated and labour-intensive shows the amount of hard work it has taken to reach your current position. Even though you may feel that you have just been lucky or made the best of things, your unconscious awareness has had a quiet purpose in guiding you to where you are now. The people travelling on foot and without mechanized transport imply that using your fundamental energy and drive has resulted in your progress. The lack of contemporary technology suggests you have had to use your resourcefulness to communicate your needs and make things happen. Although you may take your past for granted, your talents have played a large part in creating your current circumstances.

Action

This dream is a timely reminder that your past experiences have played a major role in shaping where you are currently in your waking life. It may seem as if the person you used to be is a distant memory but you still have access to all the experience and insight that you had available in the past. Although it can be easy to ignore your history as you look to your future, you shouldn't be afraid to draw on your experiences as you explore the exciting new possibilities offered by future opportunities.

Background

We are fascinated by events of the past and enjoy commemorating them in our monuments and traditions. When we study history, we often like to look at the chain of events that led to a particular historic moment, and wonder if the event would have still occurred with the omission of one of these steps. This fixation with cause and effect often leads us to believe that events could not have unfolded in any other way. Being more aware of the decisions that we take in our lives, however, means we can use past experiences to help shape our chosen futures.

80. KIDNAPPED BY A GANG

Dream

You are overwhelmed by a group of gangsters and they kidnap you, taking you to their hideout where they try to force you to join them. The gang members seem to be familiar with you and your life, and they often attempt to blackmail you. Their pretext is that you owe them some money or perhaps they witnessed a minor misdemeanour you committed. In return for their silence, they often ask you to commit crimes for them. They may place unnecessary demands on you as they threaten to hold you or your family hostage.

Meaning

Dreaming of being kidnapped by a gang suggests you have become involved with a group of people in waking life that seem to be making unfair demands on your time and resources. Although you feel a loyalty towards this group, you also feel they often seem to force you into doing things that you would rather not do. This tends to happen most often in family situations where you can sometimes feel coerced into unwelcome activities and it seems that other family members are controlling your individual freedom in some way. Family members can also try to influence you by playing on your sense of loyalty to them and by making life uncomfortable if you appear to be disloyal in any way.

This can seem like emotional blackmail but even though this group seems to be limiting your freedom, it also gives you a sense of security, which is why it can be so hard to escape from them. You can also sense a debt of gratitude to your family and this can make you feel as if you owe them something, particularly if they have ignored indiscretions and mistakes that you have made. The feeling of being kidnapped can also occur if you feel that you are being held hostage by your family's expectations of you. As well as families, this can happen in other tight-knit groups where you feel the group's interests are different from your own, causing a conflict of your loyalties.

Action

The message from this dream is that you need to place the expectations and influences of your family into a wider perspective. Although you want to respect your family, you also need to be able to make your own choices and take full responsibility for your own decisions. The more responsibly you behave, the more freedom you will have to be loyal to yourself and to honour your needs. As you realize that you are the person responsible for meeting your own expectations, you will liberate yourself from feeling trapped by the expectations of others.

Background

Although most of us have no direct experience of dealing with gangsters, such as Mafia mobsters, we have a rich cultural awareness through films like *The Godfather Trilogy* and television shows such as *The Sopranos*. The basis of each Mafia organization is a particular family or clan and, like the Mafia, many families have their informal and unspoken codes of conduct and honour. These usually involve expectations of unconditional loyalty to one another and often include a code of silence or *omerta* concerning certain taboo subjects that aren't spoken about outside the family.

81. ATTACKED BY A DOG

Dream

A dog that seems very familiar and friendly suddenly starts to snarl and growl at you. Its aggressiveness frightens you and you retreat. The dog keeps advancing towards you and starts nipping at your arms or legs. As you try and calm the dog down, it launches a full-scale attack and sinks its teeth deep into you. You find it impossible to shake it off and are concerned that you might hurt the dog in some way. The dream can also involve wilder members of the dog family such as foxes, jackals, hyenas or wolves.

Meaning

A dog is traditionally a human's best friend and its appearance in a dream usually reflects your role as a loyal and loving companion in waking life. You usually give unconditional love to a partner in the hope they will return equal amounts of affection back to you. No matter how faithful and affectionate you are, however, you are often disappointed when you feel your love isn't being returned. You become angry with the object of your affections but feel that you can't say anything in case you upset him or her. Rather than being honest and open, you may act in a passive aggressive manner and begin to make nipping remarks. As your loved one retreats you sink your teeth in and hang on for dear life in case they try to get rid of you.

If the attacking dog is black, then this may be habitual behaviour and can feel quite depressing for you after a while. The fox and the jackal suggest that you feel you are being manipulated and your affections are being preyed on in a cunning and devious way. If you are attacked by a pack of hyenas then you feel people may be laughing at your attempts at affection and aren't taking you seriously enough. Being attacked by a pack of wolves usually suggests that you are being overly loyal to family members but they aren't returning the loyalty that you give so freely to them.

Action

This dream is urging you to consider the love you give to people and how it is reciprocated. Unconditional love can be a wonderful gift of generosity and trust but you are often tempted to just give your love away. This is often driven by a fear that you are somehow unlovable and this is the only way that you will ever receive any love. Instead of hounding others to provide you with unconditional love, think about how you can love yourself unconditionally. Have faith in yourself and others will always have faith in you.

Background

Dogs were one of the first animals to be domesticated by humans and reflect how we tame and accommodate our natural instincts and aggressions. Although our innate drives become domesticated as we grow up, they can easily revert to a wilder state if our affection and fidelity are ignored. Like dogs, we are social animals who bond through loyalty and by supporting each other, as we pursue common goals. In the same way as our canine companions, we humans have a fundamental need to be part of a social group, which provides us with companionship, protection, and the opportunity to play together.

82. IMMERSED IN WATER

Dream

You step into the water and sink down until you are fully immersed. The water may be in a bath or a swimming pool, or you may be bathing in a river or the sea. You relax but then suddenly panic as your head slips underwater and you can't breathe. Even though you are in shallow water, you can't touch the bottom with your feet and you are terrified to open your mouth in case you flood your lungs. Sometimes you are sure you are about to drown but then you realize that you can breathe underwater.

Meaning

If you dream of being immersed in water, then there is a situation in your waking life where you feel that you are becoming deeply involved emotionally. Water usually represents your feelings in your dreams and stepping into water shows that you are entering into quite emotional circumstances. Sinking down into the water suggests that you are immersing yourself in your feelings and responding to what you experience at a purely emotional level. A very personal situation is usually symbolized by a bath, while a swimming pool usually shows your work life is involved. Bathing in a river indicates that this might be quite a moving experience and being in the sea shows that you are becoming emotionally involved in some wider life issues.

Your head symbolizes your thoughts and your ability to analyse the situation from a rational perspective, so if your head slips under water, your thoughts are becoming overwhelmed by your emotions. Breathing is an indication of your capacity to express your ideas logically and not being able to breathe suggests that you are struggling to put your feelings into words. Being unable to touch the bottom with your feet reflects that you are starting to feel out of your depth and are finding it difficult to stand up for yourself. You may be terrified to open your mouth in case you say the wrong thing and become even more deeply involved. Breathing underwater shows that you are starting to feel more comfortable with your emotions and are able to express your feelings easily.

Action

This dream is reflecting that your current situation is making you far more aware of your feelings. Your emotional currents usually run quite deeply so it can be a shock to your system to be plunged into these apparently irrational circumstances. Your natural reaction might be to panic as these waves of emotion sweep over you, but this can often result in you

sinking even deeper into an unfathomable mood. Instead of panicking, try to relax as much as possible. The more you can go with the flow, the more successfully you will navigate this sensitive situation.

Background

Much of our language about being emotionally involved in a situation is based on water and how we deal with being immersed in it. If we are in a situation where we have lost control of our feelings, we might say that we are *'in too deep'* or are *'trying to keep our head above water'*. When we try to keep something going in challenging emotional circumstances, we speak of *'trying to keep it afloat'* or prevent it *'from going under'*. Those who are particularly heavy snorers or suffer from sleep apnoea can also experience this dream.

83. MEETING AN OLD FRIEND

Dream

You are pleased to bump into an old friend that you haven't seen for years and years. Although you used to be very close, you just drifted apart somehow. It was always easy for you to spend time with your companion and you were invariably very relaxed in their company. Your friend also had a number of qualities you admire and you could always rely on them if you found yourself stuck in a difficult situation. You were sure that no matter what happened, your friend would always be there for you and vice versa.

Meaning

When you dream of meeting an old friend, you are becoming reacquainted with a personal quality of your own that you have somehow lost touch with. Your friend usually embodied this characteristic in waking life and you are using them to symbolize this particular aspect of yourself. The reappearance of your acquaintance suggests you need to reconnect with this distinctive quality to deal with an issue in your current circumstances. It may be that you are often quite impetuous and your friend was a calming influence, so your deeper, wiser self is suggesting that you should be calmer. On the other hand, it might be that you are the calm one and your friend was inspiring and motivating, and so you are encouraging yourself to take a chance.

If your friend is helping you out of a precarious situation, this means there is some tension in your waking life, which can be resolved by you having the courage to display the qualities you associate with your pal. It may appear as if your companion is ignoring you and this suggests you are ignoring this particular aspect of yourself. Your old mate may also have had a particular talent or skill you admired but didn't have the opportunity to express at the time. Although it may seem strange to start expressing it now, it is a natural part of yourself that you have been neglecting. By exploring this skill you can become better acquainted with your talents.

Action

The message from this dream is that you have a forgotten talent or personal quality, and would enjoy becoming reacquainted with it. Your current situation is an ideal opportunity to express this talent. You may feel slightly awkward about displaying

your abilities in public, however, and would prefer someone else to do it instead. By getting in contact with your dormant talent, you can connect with yourself at a much deeper level. Although it may seem a little uncomfortable at first, you soon begin to realize the true value of this forgotten part of yourself.

Background

We tend to choose our friends at a quite unconscious and instinctive level, and are usually drawn towards them because they have qualities that we admire and talents that complement ours. As we progress through life, our friends may come and go but the significance of the shared connections remains. A friend is someone you can confide in and reveal a vulnerable part of yourself by sharing a confidence. The word *'confide'* comes from the Latin *con fidere*, meaning *'with faith'*, and a friend affirms your faith in yourself as you confidently discover your unique qualities.

84. DERELICT HOUSE

Dream

You are shocked when you return to your house to find it derelict with the walls crumbling. Although you hadn't realized it was in such a state of disrepair, you can't believe you have let your house degenerate this much. You want to try and repair it but feel that you don't have the resources and the skills. It all feels so insecure and there may be wobbly floorboards, holes in the roof, peeling wallpaper and broken windows. You stand outside on the rubble, feeling sure that the walls are about to collapse. Often there is a solid new house standing nearby.

Meaning

When you dream of a derelict house there is some aspect of yourself that you are neglecting in waking life. A house usually symbolizes yourself and the more solid and secure the house appears, the more sure and secure you feel in yourself. It often comes as a surprise when you find your house has become derelict and this shows that you have been unaware that you have not been paying attention to yourself. The crumbling walls suggest that you are feeling a bit run down and are unable to really stand up for what you believe in. Wobbly floors indicate that you are unsure of where you stand in a particular situation and are uncertain of your next steps.

Windows reflect your perceptions of particular issues and broken windows show that you feel you need to piece some more information together to have a clearer view of what is really happening. The roof represents how secure you feel in your thinking and you may be worried that there are some gaps in your knowledge. The missing walls mean that you need to establish clear boundaries between your needs and the needs of others. This is echoed in the derelict rooms that suggest you spend more time looking after other people than you do looking after yourself. The solid new house nearby shows how secure and complete you might feel if you just changed your position and viewpoint slightly.

Action

This dream is drawing your attention to the fact that you are ignoring some personal gifts and unique talents. It can be

easy to neglect your abilities because they often don't seem as important to you as the needs of other people. The less attention you pay to your needs, the more run down you will feel, and consequently you will be less effective at looking after the needs of others. The best way to ensure that you can accommodate everyone's needs is to establish clear boundaries with them. The firmer these boundaries, the more secure you will all feel.

Background

We often associate our homes with our continuing security and happiness, using phrases like *'safe as houses'* and *'feeling right at home'*. Although we spend much of our time and money on home-improvement plans, we tend to pay a lot less attention to our individual wellbeing. It can be much easier to embark on DIY projects that might increase the value of our house, rather than spending time on increasing our sense of self-worth. In the same way that a house requires regular attention to maintain its value, so we need to ensure we maintain our commitment to ourselves.

85. ABDUCTED BY ALIENS

Dream

Alien abduction dreams often begin by having strange feelings of anxiety. Everything around you may appear to be normal but you know that something isn't quite right. You feel that the people around you might be aliens and they are about to abduct you. Although they appear normal you realize they are

other life forms in human disguise. You try to communicate with them but they don't seem to understand you and force you to go with them. Even if you escape or are released you still feel that the aliens are using advanced technology to watch you.

Meaning

Dreaming about aliens indicates you are experiencing situations in your waking life that often seem quite alien and unfamiliar to you. Being abducted suggests that you feel you have no control over the situation and are being forced to do things by other people. People who have moved into an unfamiliar new job or community, usually in a foreign country, often experience this dream. Although the new people you meet seem quite normal, they have their own culture and customs and these can seem like a completely different world to you. It may feel as if you are being forced to fit in with their cultural constraints and have no opportunity of working in your normal way.

These new people may also have their own language and jargon, which can make it difficult for you to communicate with them. Being confronted by alien technology reflects that you have a possible need to learn how to use new systems and procedures in these unusual circumstances. The reason that you find yourself in this unfamiliar situation, however, is that you have an unconscious need to explore new opportunities and this often reveals unexplored areas of yourself. Some of these parts of your character may seem unfamiliar to begin with, but the more that you explore them, the more they become a vital and integrated part of your inner world.

Action

This dream is an invitation to explore parts of your self that may seem unknown and unfamiliar to you. Although this can seem unsettling for you, it forces you to look beyond the areas of your life that are more comfortable and commonplace. These changes may seem scary but they are also an opportunity to learn new skills and to find out more about where you want to go in life. Even though you might not be remotely interested in finding out more about yourself, all you have to do is be open to new experiences and make the most of unexpected opportunities.

Background

Alien abduction seems like quite a modern theme but our ancestors used to dream of angels and spirits taking over their bodies and spiriting them away. The word *'nightmare'* is derived from *night maere*, an evil spirit that was believed to abduct the dreamer. Although the idea of aliens became more prevalent in the 1950s with the advent of orbital flight and the realities of space travel, many human societies have experience of invading foreigners who have alien customs and languages. Even though these invaders may have exerted unwelcome control on the indigenous people, they often introduced new technology and a wider view of the world.

86. CONFINED TO THE KITCHEN

Dream

Your kitchen is really hot and humid, and you seem to be stuck inside it with no way out. It is very cramped, with a large wooden table in the centre, and the furniture is often heavy and old-fashioned. You are finding it very difficult to move around and have to manoeuvre past pots and pans that are boiling over. All the work surfaces are sticky and messy, and the cooking smells can be quite overpowering. You seem to be preparing lots and lots of food but none of it seems to be for you.

Meaning

When you dream that you are confined to your kitchen, you feel you are stuck in some sort of nurturing role in your waking life. The rooms in your house symbolize the different parts of your character, and the kitchen reflects your ability to nurture yourself and other people by creating nourishing and fulfilling experiences. Although you would like to move on from this role, it seems as if there is no way out and you may feel quite hot and bothered. Furniture in dreams often represents habits and behavioural patterns, so old-fashioned furniture shows this may be a habitual obligation, which is weighing you down. Tables usually signify relationships so it seems as if you are feeling obliged to look after other people.

Finding it difficult to move around suggests these obligations are cramping your style and this is leaving you feeling frustrated.

The boiling pots and pans reflect these simmering frustrations but you are finding it difficult to let off steam because you are afraid of upsetting other people. Preparing food for others but not yourself shows that you are helping others to become fulfilled at your expense. This is a recipe for disaster because you would far rather be cooking up your own plans and ideas. Although you unselfishly take care of others in the hope that they will notice and appreciate your efforts, you sometimes wish other people would just look after you for a change.

Action

The message from this dream is that you are finding it difficult to look after your fundamental needs because you spend so much of your time looking after the needs of other people. Although you are accustomed to doing this and do it habitually, it often leaves you frustrated that no one seems to be taking care of you. Constantly providing for others, however, can also sometimes be a subtle way of trying to control them. Instead of always pandering to everyone else's needs, just try letting go for a change and see what happens.

Background

The kitchen is the room where we transform raw ingredients into nourishing experiences to sustain us. A lot of the imagery we use to describe our creative efforts is based on kitchen and cookery language. We speak about *'having something on the back burner'*, *'coming to the boil'* and *'cooking up a plan'*. When we feel that our efforts are going unnoticed in any part of our lives, we also use cooking language to express our frustrations. We might say that we are *'simmering with anger'*, *'reaching boiling point'* or being *'left to stew'*.

87. CHEWING GLASS

Dream

You are speaking quite normally to some friends or colleagues when you suddenly realize that your mouth is full of something sharp, like fragments of glass or razorblades. Although you try to talk quite carefully, you cut the inside of your mouth every time you speak. Blood starts to pour from your mouth and as it runs down your face, you are worried that you might swallow some of these sharp fragments. You may also be anxious that you might choke on your blood. A variation of this dream is that your mouth is full of stinging insects, such as wasps or hornets.

Meaning

If you dream about chewing glass or having a sharp object in your mouth, then you are thinking about how pointedly you sometimes communicate with other people in your waking life. In addition to your teeth, your mouth mainly consists of the soft flesh and tissue that you use to shape and express your words. Your mouth is one of the most sensitive areas of your body, so it can be a shock to realize that there is unexpected sharpness inside it. The splinters and shards, however, aren't glass but the unanticipated sharp words and pointed remarks that you often find passing through your mouth. They may seem to be just words but they are often heard as cutting remarks and can be quite wounding for others.

You may resort to using your sharp tongue when you feel threatened by other people and are trying to defend your

position. Even though you try to choose your words carefully, you can still end up hurting the other people's feelings and your barbed remarks can also wound and upset you, too. Your blood represents your deepest feelings and, although you are trying to contain them and choke them back, they keep spilling out for everyone to see. You may also be worried about your pride being wounded if you are forced to eat your words. Wasps or hornets in your mouth show similar concerns about making too many stinging remarks to other people.

Action

This dream is suggesting that you should perhaps keep your razor-like wit in check by taking a more gentle approach and accepting your vulnerabilities. Rather than feeling that you have to constantly defend your position by attacking others, try using softer words to move on from the disagreements in which you are currently involved. Maintaining an unnecessary stance can be stressful and, if you continue to present a tough, hard exterior, you will just end up shattering your fragile confidence. The right words, spoken softly, are far more powerful and inspiring than any amount of sharp criticism.

Background

Much of the language that we use to describe insults and arguments is based on metaphors of wounding and cutting. Before we had tools, our most basic method of cutting was by using our mouths and this is also the body part we use to shape and speak our words. In our contemporary culture, using our mouth continues to be one of the main ways we defend ourselves and attack others. Instead of physically biting and wounding our adversaries, however, we now use our words to pierce the defences of those people who seem to threaten us.

88. UNINVITED GUESTS

Dream

You are alone at home, relaxing and having a nice quiet time. Suddenly you begin to realize that you aren't on your own any more. You may hear voices or the sound of domestic activity as people come into the house and one or two people might pop their heads around the door of the room that you are relaxing in. When you go to investigate the noise you find your house is full of strangers and they seem to ignore you, just brushing past you. Although some of the people may be familiar, most of them seem to be total strangers.

Meaning

Dreaming of uninvited guests often indicates that you are becoming aware of a number of opportunities for growth and development in your waking life. Relaxing in your house suggests that you are feeling comfortable and at home with yourself, and are trying to enjoy some quiet time. No matter how much you try and consciously relax, however, these opportunities keep trying to attract your attention. The people entering your house symbolize these possibilities and, although you may try and ignore them, they will continue to make themselves known until you start to pay heed to them. At first, there may only seem to be one or two opportunities popping up but when you investigate these, you might start to feel overwhelmed by all the other possibilities.

The people who appear in your dreams are often reflections of various aspects of your character. Friends and family tend to symbolize those characteristics you are familiar with, whereas strangers usually represent areas of your character that you would like to explore and develop further. The strangers who seem to ignore you are reflecting the fact that you are ignoring a great deal of your potential and you need to share your abilities with a much wider audience. The more you retreat into your individual space and private world, the more difficult it is for your talents to be stimulated. Although it seems an intrusion into your privacy, you are actually reminding yourself of your untapped potential.

Action

This dream is drawing your attention to unexplored parts of your character that could potentially be very useful to you. It can be easy to retreat into a relaxed and comfortable routine but this can often prevent you from participating in more fulfilling opportunities. The more you try to resist individual opportunities, the more restless your relaxation time will become. Although it is valuable to claim time for yourself, where you can relax and reflect, it is good to balance this with stepping out of your comfort zone and experiencing what else might be out there.

Background

Although we are social animals, we all need our private space. The anthropologist Edward T Hall introduced the idea of Proxemics, which describes how we all try to claim and maintain our personal space, even in crowded situations. Our comfort zones, the areas in which we feel no anxiety or are able to cope with feelings of anxiety, often echo our personal space. The most successful people tend to be those who are

consistently able to go beyond their comfort zone and although it may seem safer to stay where we feel comfortable, it can also create a false sense of security.

89. SURROUNDED BY SNAKES

Dream

You are making your way through some unfamiliar territory when you encounter a number of slithering and writhing snakes. They are often in a pit in front of you or surrounding you as they wriggle around on the floor. You are anxious that you might fall over and become covered in them as they crawl all over you. Some of the snakes may be rearing up and getting ready to attack by sinking their fangs into you. Others may be sliding across the ground towards you as they try to wrap you in their muscular coils.

Meaning

Dreaming of being surrounded by snakes often suggests that you are encountering a number of opportunities to transform yourself in your daily life. Although most people don't encounter actual snakes on a regular basis in their day-to-day lives, they appear regularly as slithering and sliding symbols in our dreams. Snakes symbolize opportunities for change and often represent your ability to grow and mature in waking life. Your skin represents the meeting place where your inner and outer worlds join, as it is the visible embodiment of all your actions and behaviours. In the same way that a snake sheds its skin, you also help your healthy growth by discarding aspects of your behaviour that are no longer of value to you.

Being in a pit or on the ground suggests that you have to take some practical steps forward to embrace these opportunities for transformation. Although you are concerned that you might be overwhelmed by opportunities and feel this might be your downfall, your increasing confidence will make it easier to move forward. Snakes rearing and showing their fangs suggest that you are concerned about the criticism you might receive from others as you start to transform your life. The constrictors slithering across the floor indicate that other people might be trying to constrict your freedom and give you no room to manoeuvre as you try to step into your new future. Many people are scared of change because, like a snake, it can seem threatening to their survival.

Action

This dream is alerting you to an opportunity for personal change by taking some transformative action in your waking life. You may be afraid to make this move because you know it will mean having to let go of part of your old life before you can begin to move into the new one. Letting go of old habits and self-limiting behaviours will give you more freedom for personal growth. The more you can open yourself up to these new possibilities, the more comfortable you will be in your own skin.

Background

Snakes and serpents occupy a uniquely symbolic presence in nearly all cultures. One of their main associations is with medicine and healing, and a snake can be seen entwined around the Rod of Asclepius, the symbol of a practising doctor.

Many pharmaceutical associations use the Bowl of Hygieia, symbolized by a medicine bowl with a snake wrapped around it. Snakes also symbolize transformation, as they have the ability to change their skins. We all experience the snake-like umbilical cord when we emerge into the world, as we leave our mother's skin behind and are born into our own individual skins.

90. RESTRICTED OPENING

Dream

You are trying to get somewhere but you have to squeeze through tight spaces and openings before you can reach your objective. These might be narrow tunnels or alleyways, forcing you to wriggle through doors and holes that seem far too small to fully accommodate you. The spaces you are forced into can seem like boxes and pipes, such as ventilation ducting or underground culverts. As you work your way through the labyrinthine spaces, you become concerned that you are going to get stuck and might end up jammed in an awkward and uncomfortable shape.

Meaning

Dreaming of squeezing through a tunnel or a restricted opening usually indicates that you feel your progress in waking life is being constrained in some way. You often start off in a wide and spacious place, suggesting that you feel you have lots of opportunities and the future seems wide open, but, as you advance, you find your options narrowing and you don't have room to manoeuvre. If you are in a stone tunnel or old-fashioned alleyway, then you are feeling restricted by traditional structures of old habits and unyielding authorities. The hard surfaces of the tunnel symbolize the sharply defined rules and regulations that seem to limit your freedom.

This can make you feel tightly confined and with no opportunity to stretch the rules. The small doors and holes represent opportunities and openings that don't seem big enough to get you where you want to be. Being forced into a particular space indicates that you feel you are being coerced into making decisions not in your best interests. Air ducting suggests that you have to work with some procedures that seem quite narrow-minded and culverts imply that you are being expected to behave in a particular way. Ending up jammed in an awkward and uncomfortable position shows you are concerned that you will be pressured into adopting a particular stance if you continue to follow your current path.

Action

This dream is opening you up to the possibility that you actually have more choices than you think. You may feel that the rules are written in stone and you have to jump through hoops to please other people, but these are usually self-limiting beliefs that are getting you nowhere. Instead of following the tortuous procedures laid down by others, try looking at alternative ways of attaining your objective. You can also hasten your progress by slimming down your expectations and releasing yourself from some of the obligations and burdens that may be holding you back.

Background

Much of our language around having to make hard choices is based on descriptions of restrictions. We speak about being 'stuck between a rock and a hard place', 'going through official channels', 'it's going to be a bit of a squeeze', and 'light at the end of the tunnel'. The feeling of being blocked in is expressed in phrases such as 'stuck in a dead-end job' or 'up against the wall'. Conversely, the idea of opportunity is often described in geographic terms of openness and space such as 'broad horizons' and 'wide open' possibilities.

91. BEING INTOXICATED OR ADDICTED

Dream

Although you tend to live in moderation in waking life, you find yourself completely drunk or addicted to drugs and acting irresponsibly and out of character in this dream. You feel utterly out of control and are doing things you would never normally do if you were sober. There never seems to be enough drink or drugs and the more you have, the more you want. It may be that you are a non-smoker and find yourself chain-smoking. Even though you are coughing and choking, you keep puffing away and then light up another one.

Meaning

When you dream about drinking alcohol to excess or being addicted to drugs, there is usually some situation you are trying to escape from in your waking life. You know this situation is harmful to you and spend a lot of time thinking about how you can free yourself from it. But you keep getting drawn back into

it again and again and just can't understand why. Although the dream is about a dependency on drink or drugs, your addiction in waking life is usually to a particular person. Your relationship with this person is often romantic and, even though you feel strongly attracted to them, there is an unresolved tension between you that can get out of control very quickly.

This lack of control is unsettling for you, so you may find it difficult to acknowledge whatever it is that is causing this disruption in your life. In the same way that an addict habitually craves a fix you have some deep need or desire that keeps drawing you back towards this person. Even though you know that this situation is detrimental to you in the long term, it is giving you a buzz that you just can't seem to get anywhere else. This makes it difficult for you to maintain a healthy relationship and keeps pulling you back into addictive and destructive behaviour. Although you keep trying to end the relationship, you always go back for more and it makes you feel terrible.

Action

This dream is drawing your attention to an unhealthy situation in your waking life that you habitually avoid any confrontation with. Although your fundamental need is to be in a loving and intimate relationship, you are finding it difficult to escape the feeling that somehow you are just not worth it. Rather than openly dealing with the issue, it can seem much easier to think that somehow everything will work out absolutely perfectly for you. The less that you can depend on your self-worth, however, the more dependent you will be on other people to make you feel good.

Background

When we have an unhealthy emotional dependency on someone, we often use language describing a physical

addiction. We hear phrases like *'he's a habit I just can't break'* or *'I need to go cold turkey'*. This language also appears in popular song titles such as *I Get a Kick Out of You*, *Addicted to Love*, and *Love is the Drug*. Many addictions are attempts to fulfil an emotional need in a particular physical way but this can lead to compulsive behaviour and psychological dependency until the underlying emotional need has actually been satisfied.

92. BURNING BUILDING

Dream

You see smoke in the distance and realize that a familiar building appears to be on fire. The building is often your house or workplace. It may have started out as a small blaze but now is in danger of developing into a major inferno. Often one room is completely ablaze and you fear that the fire will spread to the rest of the building. You look around for ways to extinguish the fire but everything seems to be broken or ineffectual. Although you try to get hold of the fire brigade or passers-by, no one seems to be able to help you.

Meaning

When you dream of a burning building, it often indicates the potential for a major creative transformation in your waking life. A building usually symbolizes your true identity and the type of burning building will indicate which part of your identity is open to being transformed. If it is your workplace then it is a professional change, and if it is your house, then this is quite

a personal transformation. Frictions in a close relationship can ignite this opportunity for transformation and it may be quite a volatile partnership with heated discussions and inflamed emotions. Although the initial disagreement may have been sparked off by a small difference of opinion, it has become an increasingly heated discussion and ignited an all-consuming and blazing row.

Even though the fire is only affecting one part of the building, you are worried that it will soon spread to more rooms and areas. This reflects that the original issue was quite contained and localized but you are now concerned that it has the potential to adversely affect other areas of your life. No one seems to be able to help you because only you can channel this passionate and creative energy and control what you do with it. Your uncontrolled passion can be remarkably destructive but if you can learn to harness it, it becomes a great source of power and confidence for you. Rather than being consumed by your creative impulses, you can become a warm and generous individual who can direct and catalyse powerful changes.

Action

This dream is illuminating your need to take some creative action in order to transform your current situation. No matter how fired up you may be, however, you are finding it difficult to direct your energies towards a constructive outcome. It may seem as if the best approach is to take as much heat out of the situation as you can but this may also dampen your enthusiasm for future opportunities. Rather than becoming consumed by an all-or-nothing approach, try creatively directing your energies towards a constructive and sustainable outcome that can accommodate everyone.

Background

We use houses and buildings to represent our various selves and fire has come to symbolize the process of creative transformation. Fire is a uniquely human tool that we use to transform and create, and so has come to represent our creative spirit; but as well as creating, fire also destroys. Many creative processes involve the apparent destruction of one thing to produce another. When we are at our most creative, we use phrases like *'I'm on fire'*, *'We're hot to trot'* or *'getting on like a house on fire'*.

93. BEFRIENDING A WILD ANIMAL

Dream

In this dream you are befriending a wild animal or trying to capture and tame it. The animal often seems to have the ability to talk and may have other apparently magical powers. You are very keen to get closer to the animal by stroking it and speaking to it. Even though the animal seems quite wild, you aren't scared or trying to run away from it. The animal may seem shy or uncooperative at first but as you gain its trust, you find that it really begins to communicate with you, often offering valuable advice and insight.

Meaning

When you dream about making friends with a wild animal, you are becoming more aware and appreciative of your instinctive

nature in waking life. Animals usually symbolize your unconscious needs and your natural impulses, which you may often try to tame and keep under control because you are concerned that they will break free and cause havoc. The animal's ability to talk reflects that you are starting to be able to give voice to your true nature and want to get closer to this aspect of yourself because it seems very appealing to you. Although it may take a while to gain the animal's trust, this reflects the fact that it can often take time for you to trust your instincts.

The nature of the animal you are befriending will indicate what part of your unconscious nature you are starting to accept more. Horses represent the personal urges and passions that you are trying to harness and put to work for you. Elephants show how you are becoming more familiar with your personal strengths and the power of your life experiences. Camels suggest that you are able to persevere and endure adversity in order to reach where you really need to get to in your life. Bears emphasize your independence and loyalty to others. Becoming more friendly with a marine animal, such as a dolphin or a whale, reflects that you are becoming much more in touch with your emotions.

Action

This dream is helping you to connect more deeply with your creative instincts and impulses. It can be easy to be afraid of your natural or instinctive behaviour because you are anxious that it might carry you away and cause you some harm. Your instincts, however, can be enormously powerful at helping you in situations where rational analysis just doesn't make any sense of what is really going on. The more that you can pay attention to your instinctive awareness, the more likely you are to sense all the subtle possibilities that are happening around you.

Background

We tend not to appear in our dreams until about the age of three to four. Instead our dreams are filled with animals as we explore our instinctive and impulsive natures. Most of our initial learning of words and speech comes from animal identification and the sounds they make. As we develop into adults, we usually suppress much of our instinctive and impulsive natures but they are seen most clearly in what we create. Creativity and creature come from the same Latin word *creare*, meaning *'to make and produce'*, and what we create usually reveals our unique natures.

94. TRAPPED IN PRISON

Dream

Surrounded by steel bars and metal furniture, with minimal facilities and under constant supervision, you find yourself locked up in prison for some reason. Although you aren't quite sure why you are there, you know that you have some time to serve. You are often in solitary confinement and time drags really slowly, strictly controlled by the prison routine. The prison warders are unsympathetic to your plight and have no interest in your life beyond the prison. You try to convince them that you haven't done anything wrong but they won't listen and keep you locked up.

Meaning

Dreaming of being trapped in prison often indicates that you feel that you have lost some of your freedom to act independently

in your waking life. This can result in you relying on others to make your decisions and to permit your actions – something that can often happen if you feel stuck in a particular role in your workplace or in a relationship. Steel bars show that you think there is something barring your progress and the minimal facilities suggest you don't feel you have the resources you need to be more comfortable. The feeling of having time to serve is caused by having made a commitment to a job or a person in waking life and then waiting for them to release you from it.

This can be quite lonely for you because you feel that you have no one to really talk to, while your habitual routines prevent you from expressing your fears and doubts about your situation. The prison warders symbolize your sense of duty and the reason they ignore you is because your prison is usually of your making. You don't want to let others down by releasing yourself from your commitments, so you end up feeling trapped by your misplaced sense of obligation. Even though you are trying to convince yourself that you are doing the right thing, the commitments you have made have left you feeling confined and solitary. The key to releasing yourself is just to open up and say what you really think.

Action

This dream is obliging you to be more decisive and begin taking charge of your life again. Although you may feel trapped, a prison is also a very secure environment and so you may be locking yourself away in a safe place rather than taking the risk of venturing out into the unknown. The commitments and obligations you make to others are often a way of feeling needed and accepted but this can lead to situations where you have become overly dependent on others. The more responsibility that you take for your decisions, however, the more freedom you will enjoy.

Background

Our first experiences of feeling trapped in a place where we don't want to be often start at school. While we would rather be running around and enjoying our freedom, we are forced to sit though dull experiences and lessons that are often tedious. We have to work to a timetable and a syllabus and we know that we are free to go once we have done our time. This feeling of being trapped often extends into our corporate lives where we can feel stuck in particular roles and routines.

95. EMPTY WORKPLACE

Dream

You turn up to work at your usual time and place but are surprised that none of your colleagues seem to be around. When you try to enter the building or site, your swipe card or security code no longer works. Your usual workplace equipment might also be missing and you spend a lot of time looking for the tools that you normally use. These tools may also have been replaced with shiny new equipment just waiting to be utilized but you don't feel that you have permission to operate it. You try to ask for help but no one seems to respond to your requests.

Meaning

Dreaming of an empty workplace can indicate that you feel your professional abilities aren't being fully recognized and appreciated by other people in your waking life. The workplace often symbolizes your capacity to productively employ your unique talents and create value by using them. None of your colleagues being around at the usual time and place suggests that you feel that your abilities are routinely unacknowledged and that no one else is really aware of the value of the work you do. Not being able to enter particular areas because of your swipe card or security code shows that you know you have the required professional credentials, but are being denied access to new opportunities for some reason.

Missing equipment and tools also show that you feel that you have the ability to be useful and productive but are struggling to find the opportunity to use your skills. Shiny new equipment represents new and exciting opportunities but not having permission to use it suggests you lack the confidence to explore these possibilities. Although it can seem like everyone is ignoring your abilities, this is often a result of you neglecting your skills and not valuing your talent highly enough. The workplace is where you take the raw material of your raw talent and create something valuable from it. Unless you can recognize and appreciate your talents and draw attention to them, it can be difficult for others to actually realize your true value.

Action

To make the most of this dream, you need to place more value on your skills and talents in waking life. It can be easy to dismiss your abilities as being ordinary because you are so comfortable

and confident with them. The best way to have your unique abilities acknowledged and appreciated by others is to begin recognizing and realizing the true value of your skills. The more you value your abilities, the more confident you will be about using your talents in unusual situations and this will open up a new world of employment possibilities for you.

Background

Although we may seem to choose our jobs rationally based on the terms and conditions offered to us, the fundamental quality we look for in a job is that it is meaningful work with a purpose. Giving us a meaningful purpose in life is one of the most valuable benefits of a job because it reflects our value and self-worth beyond any financial and material rewards that we receive. Although we may look forward to retiring or moving on, we very often lose our sense of purpose in life if we have no meaningful work to inspire us.

96. LOST YOUR SHOES

Dream

Somehow you have lost your shoes and are outside walking around in your socks or bare feet. You can often find yourself walking through a big city, wondering how you will be able to walk to your destination without any shoes. After a while you realize that you don't really need your footwear but are concerned what other people will think of you. Wearing shoes would sometimes be more comfortable, however, as the ground is rough or all wet and muddy. You were sure you had more shoes but it seems you have lost your only pair.

Meaning

When you dream about losing your shoes, you are usually concerned about your ability to stand up for what you believe in. Your feet symbolize the foundation of any position that you hold and represent the principles and values that help to keep you grounded in reality. What you wear on your feet represents your ability to protect these fundamental principles and also the steps that you take to put them into action. Shoes are among the most personal items of clothing and, like your values, have to fit just right or you will feel uncomfortable. Your shoes also represent your individuality and so losing your shoes indicates that you feel you are losing your identity in some way.

Due to the fact that your shoes represent your identity so individually, they tend to reflect your current social status as well. Losing your shoes can also indicate that you feel you have lost your social standing in some way. This can often happen when you have recently left a particular relationship or work situation and are concerned that people might ignore you. Although you may think that you can progress just as easily on your own, it is often good to have the firm support of others when the going gets rough. Thinking that you have only one pair of shoes suggests that you have been relying too much on one particular standpoint to provide you with what you need.

Action

This dream is indicating the steps that you need to take to help re-establish your standing in a particular situation. Although this might feel quite uncomfortable for you, it is an opportunity that will help you to become far more aware of what you really value. It is also a chance to think about the positions of others in this situation and consider what it would be like to stand in their shoes. The more that you realize what you really value and how that supports you, the easier it is to stand up for yourself and really walk your talk.

Background

Our ancestors starting wearing shoes about 40,000 years ago, using simple wrappings and foot bags to protect their feet. Since then, they have become a vital fashion accessory and our shoes have come to reflect our desirability, our status and our wealth. Rather than judging each other by our actions and deeds, we often judge a person by the shoes that they wear. Smart and shiny shoes can often indicate the wearer is behaving formally with a more polished approach. Mud-spattered work boots may imply a more grounded and practical outlook.

97. OVERWHELMED BY VERMIN

Dream

You find yourself in a place overwhelmed by vermin and although this can be your home, it is very often your workplace. It can seem like a plague and the animals are usually rodents or insects, which are doing physical harm to your surroundings or possessions. You try to find ways of putting traps down or getting rid of the infestation but it just gets worse and worse,

as they are eating food, gnawing cables and spreading disease and destruction. No matter how often you try and stop them, they keep multiplying and overrunning everything.

Meaning

Dreaming of being overwhelmed by vermin often indicates that small problems and anxieties seem to be mounting up in your waking life. Individually, these pesky events appear to be quite unremarkable and inconsequential, but these little worries can build up into bigger problems that are far more disturbing and destructive. The vermin in your dream probably represent some seemingly minor issues and concerns that you have about a certain situation. Although you are trying to ignore what is happening, all these small anxieties are accumulating into major worries, which are eating away at your self-confidence. Even though you are managing to deal with these apparently trivial problems one by one, it seems that you aren't getting to the source of what is causing all your concerns.

It might seem that you are being overwhelmed by minor irritations but this is often caused by not looking at the bigger situation. Trying to deal with individual problems one by one prevents you from resolving the situation completely because you are spending all your time focusing on the small annoyances instead of dealing with the fundamental cause of the problem. This can result in you feeling trapped and you may become very frustrated because you feel that any work that you do will be compromised, no matter how carefully you cultivate your talents. Until you can clear these problems up, they will always plague your efforts and prevent you from achieving healthy productivity.

Action

This dream is making you aware that you seem to spend most of your time having to deal with the smaller tactical issues in a particular situation. The time that you spend dealing with these less significant issues, however, is denying you the opportunity to make the strategic decisions that would completely resolve the problems. This often occurs because you feel comfortable dealing diligently with small problems but lack confidence in your ability to deal with larger issues. By having the courage to confront the source of your problems, you can rid yourself of these gnawing anxieties once and for all.

Background

When we speak about frustrations that constantly afflict us, we use phrases like *'it's such a pest'*, *'the fly in the ointment'*, *'being pestered'*, or *'smelling a rat'*. The word *'vermin'* comes from the Latin *verminatus,* which has the dual meaning of being *'infested with maggots'* and also *'racked with pain'*. When we are plagued by anxieties, it can really feel as if there is something eating away at us inside. Although we may hope that the Pied Piper will come along and remove the infestation, the best way to eradicate our frustrations is to deal with the source of our anxieties.

98. BEING INVISIBLE

Dream

Everything seems normal but no one appears to recognize you. Even though you can see yourself, you seem to be invisible to everyone else. You may be at a social function or in a familiar situation with all of your friends but none of them actually notice you are there. Every time you try to join in, other people blank you or talk over you and sometimes it seems as if they are looking straight through you. You may realize that you are all in some kind of danger but nobody pays any attention to you as you try to alert them.

Meaning

Dreaming of being invisible to others usually suggests that you aren't making yourself as visible as you would like to be in waking life. This is often caused by a situation where you are working behind the scenes to make something happen but no one seems to recognize your work. Although it would be easy to blame others for not noticing your efforts, this dream is often about allowing yourself and your talents to be acknowledged by others. However, it can be difficult for others to be appreciative of your qualities if you find it difficult to appreciate your own talents. This is often because you lack confidence in your abilities and are afraid that you might fail and be criticized for it.

Lacking confidence means that you often tend to put the needs of others before your needs. By serving others you think you will appear valuable to them and this will somehow be rewarded by

their recognition of you. You don't draw attention to your efforts and so it is unsurprising that they aren't recognized in return. Rather than making a fuss, you find it easier to step back and just fade into the background. The danger that you are trying to alert people to is that you are in jeopardy of ignoring your uniqueness. The best way to encourage others to pay attention to you is to start paying attention to your talents and making them much more visible to others.

Action

This dream is encouraging you to make yourself more visible so that others can recognize your talents and your real value. Although it may feel more comfortable not to be the centre of attention, it also means that most of your efforts usually go unnoticed by other people. You may feel that concealing your true need for recognition is the most appropriate action but it also denies you the opportunity to fully express your uniqueness. The more that you can openly display your abilities, then the more obvious your value will be to yourself and others.

Background

How visible we feel often depends on our perceived status in society or a social grouping. If we feel we are low-status nobodies, then we can feel invisible, whereas high-status individuals are nearly always the centre of attention. As well as occurring in social situations, this can often happen in potentially close and intimate relationships where one partner may feel ignored and say *'They don't even know that I exist'*. The more attention we pay to something, the more obvious it becomes, and the more we pay attention to ourselves, the more obvious our talents become.

99. TAKING A SHOWER

Dream

You feel hot and sticky and you want to take a long invigorating shower to freshen up. As you look for a shower, you find that all the cubicles are occupied or the shower heads are in really strange places. Eventually you find an empty cubicle but it is dark and difficult to stand up in. The shower controls are very stiff and squeaky, and when you turn it on you only get a trickle of water. The water often starts as a dirty and dark-coloured stream but usually clears to a clean and refreshing flow.

Meaning

When you dream about taking a shower you are often reflecting on an emotional situation in your waking life where you would like to clear a few things up because it seems a bit messy. This is usually caused by some tension in a relationship where you are finding it difficult to say what you need to, which is making you feel slightly guilty. Water symbolizes your feelings and so having a shower often represents a refreshing outpouring of emotions, which can help you to make a clean start in these particular circumstances. Looking for a shower indicates that you are trying to find the right opportunity to open up your feelings and perhaps let off some steam.

Finding the showers already occupied suggests that you often tend to put other people's feelings ahead of your own and you spend far more time listening to their problems than you do expressing your feelings. The shower heads in strange places show that you perhaps feel that it isn't the right time or place to say what you really think. When you do eventually find the opportunity to express your feelings, you can find it difficult to stand up for yourself and you may seem quite negative and critical. You may start by communicating in a rather inflexible manner and find it difficult to say what you really want to. Nevertheless, the more that you open up, then the clearer things become for you.

Action

This dream is suggesting that you should come clean about an emotional situation that has been making you feel guilty. You may be finding it difficult to clarify where you really stand and are looking for an appropriate time to do it. The longer that you wait for your chance, however, the worse things seem to become. Rather than endlessly waiting for the perfect moment, sometimes you just need to let it all come flooding out. Although it may seem a bit messy at the time, it usually clears the situation up for all concerned.

Background

The language we use around feelings of guilt and emotional confusion often implies that we *'feel dirty'*, or that *'things are really messy'*. When we want to move on beyond this confused situation, we speak of wanting to *'clear things up'* and *'make a fresh start'*. Although we can clean our outsides by relaxing in the bath, this passive approach does not usually work when we are trying to come clean with someone. A shower symbolizes an active cleansing process with an outpouring of feelings, which helps us to start afresh.

100. TRAVELLING TO THE FUTURE

Dream

You are still the same age but have somehow travelled into the future. People are talking into strange shiny devices and wearing futuristic clothes but still seem to have the same disagreements as they do in the present. You are intrigued by all the new technology and are eager to use it to advance yourself. Although it seems bewildering at first, you soon start to understand how it all works. Even though it is the future, you keep encountering problems from the past that you thought would have been resolved by now.

Meaning

When you dream of travelling to the future you are considering how you can advance yourself and realize some of your ambitions in waking life. The future is usually represented in dreams by the level of technological advancement and the more revolutionary the technology, the further forward you seem to have travelled in time. The communication devices symbolize how people relate to each other and their clothes represent the behaviour they exhibit to each other. Although their attire is shiny and futuristic, it seems that people are still arguing and falling out in the same way as they do in the present. Even though you thought technology would solve everything, human characteristics and behavioural patterns with all their habits and flaws still prevail.

Relying on technological advances to take you into the future indicates that you often look for external answers to advance your ambitions. No matter how much you rely on outside assistance, however, you need to travel to your inner self to really move your hopes and aspirations forward. Your journey to the future may also show that you feel unfulfilled in the present and it is time to move on. Although you would like an easy and labour-saving way to do this, it usually takes a commitment of time and effort to enable you to move forward. The further you travel on your journey of inner discovery, the sooner you will step into your ideal future.

Action

This dream is inviting you to explore what your future holds and to consider it in greater detail. You might presume that everything will be much better in the future but you know that you will need to shift some of your perspectives to really make it happen. Rather than relying on external assistance, you can use your imagination to travel through time and envision the future you want to have. As soon as you start to do this, your future often begins to manifest itself in small ways that begin to appear as you build up your new world.

Background

The future used to be portrayed in stories as an idealized utopia with people flying around using jet packs and having access to free energy and unlimited space travel. The more that we travel into the future, however, the more dystopian it seems to have become. Books such as *Brave New World* by Aldous Huxley and films like Ridley Scott's *Blade Runner* show us that, even with the most modern technologies, we still have to communicate at a human level. The most fulfilling way to travel

into our futures is often by understanding the identities, needs and beliefs of our fellow human travellers.

ABOUT

Dreaming

Using Your Dreams

Although understanding the meanings of your dreams gives you a much wider awareness of who you are and what you need and believe, it can sometimes seem like a real challenge to use these half-glimpsed dream messages in the reality of your waking life. However, the more you open yourself up to the stories that you unconsciously create, the easier it will become to remember your dreams and put them to work for you. Rather than focusing on a specific symbol, it is best to work with the dream patterns you generate. These patterns are the most authentic reflection of what is actually happening in your day-to-day life.

The 100 dream patterns described here suggest a variety of steps that you can take to put your dreams into action. You will also find these fundamental themes connecting with other patterns and constructing larger and more complex stories. You can use these larger patterns to build wider areas of understanding and be more definitive about the actions you take in waking life. Even in the most complex and seemingly bizarre dreams you will find these basic patterns, and can use them to form a firm foundation for understanding the messages that you are unconsciously creating for yourself.

For example, if you dream that you are *'Being Chased'*, then there is usually a tension that you have to resolve in waking life. If you dream that you are *'Falling'*, it shows there is some situation where you need to relax and let go in daily life. Having a dream where you are being chased and end up falling down a cliff suggests that you can start to resolve some personal tensions by relaxing and just letting go in a particular situation. When you start to do this, you may find yourself *'Flying'* as you release yourself from a number of self-imposed obligations and feel a weight lifted from your shoulders.

You can also use this awareness in the other direction, from your waking life into your dream life. If you spend a lot of time trying to pack as much into your life as possible, but are sometimes anxious that you are missing out on bigger opportunities, then it is quite likely you will have dreams like *'Endless Packing'* and *'Missing a Plane'*. These themes will often combine in dreams about cramming items into your luggage, as you try to make it to the airport on time. As you see these confirmations in your dream patterns, you can begin to take the actions associated with them in your waking life.

Your unconscious awareness is one of the most powerful personal resources you possess. It continually shines out around you, reflecting back cues and clues that can help you to make sense of your day-to-day life. When you experience being drawn towards something or having an intuitive hunch, then you are using your unconscious awareness. If you find yourself thinking that something is just a coincidence, or that you have been really lucky, then you have probably unconsciously recognized an opportunity. Your dreams and your unconscious awareness can help you enormously in waking life, but a dream is just a dream until you put it into action.

Lights, Pillow, Action!

Putting your dreams into action begins before you even turn out the light and settle down to sleep. A fundamental part of understanding your dreams is actually remembering them. Many people are utterly convinced that they don't actually dream, but everyone dreams because it is fundamental to our psychological health and physiological wellbeing. We dream most vividly during rapid eye movement episodes, and when deprived of dream-rich REM sleep, we quickly become confused and unable to cope with the simplest tasks in daily life. Although you naturally tend to forget your dreams so that you can quickly adjust to your waking reality, there are a number of steps you can take to help you remember your dreams.

The first step in remembering your dreams is to create a relaxed sleeping environment. It can be easy for your waking life to intrude upon your dream life, so try and clear all unnecessary distractions from your bedroom. Televisions, computers and gadgets in the bedroom can overstimulate a tired mind, making it difficult for you to enter a deep and restful sleep. Make sure that you feel as comfortable and relaxed as possible and then, as you lay your head on the pillow ready to fall asleep, say to yourself *'Tonight, I will remember my dreams'*. This will make you much more likely to retain your dream imagery and experiences.

When you do wake up, keep your eyes closed and try not to move your body for a minute or so. Stay absolutely still, because as soon as you begin to change body position, your dream imagery will start to fade. Within five minutes, about half of it will have faded back into your unconscious awareness and within ten minutes, most of it will have slipped away. This can be a challenge if you have to jump out of bed immediately but if you do have the luxury of lying still for a minute, then just allow any images and feelings from your dreams to emerge into your waking consciousness.

It may be difficult to see any images at first, so concentrate on your feelings instead. Are you feeling happy, anxious, exhilarated, frustrated? As you become more aware of your feelings, then imagery from your dreams will start to appear. These images may seem to be quite fleeting and vague to begin with but, as you let them come into your awareness, you should be able to start connecting them together into a coherent dream recall. The more you do this, then the more comfortable you will become doing it, and you will find it becomes easier and easier to remember your dreams.

It may seem unusual that we forget our dreams so easily, even though they can give us a much deeper understanding and wider awareness of our waking life. The evolutionary reason that we forget our dreams is so that we can quickly distinguish between our dreams and waking reality when we wake up. In our past, we needed to quickly step from our dreaming caves into an instant conscious reality so we could deal with potentially life-threatening situations. As our ancestors began painting their hunting dreams on their cave walls, however, much of our existence became based on our shared symbols, and so remembering our dreams and the symbols they speak has become evolutionarily selective.

Influencing Your Dreams

Even though your dreams may seem to be experiences that you spontaneously create, you can also specifically influence your dreams in a number of ways. One of the easiest ways to do this is to have some positive intentions for your dreaming. As you lay your head on the pillow and affirm that you will remember your dreams, choose one particular thing to dream about. This can be a special area of interest or something you feel is causing you tension in waking life. Problems that seem imponderable using rational logic are often easily solved using the innate wisdom of your unconscious awareness.

Understanding the stages of dreaming will also help you to influence your dreams. The first stage in your dreaming cycle is known as the hypnagogic stage. This happens as you begin to relax and drift off to sleep. It usually takes the form of apparently random flashes of imagery, most of it drawn from the day's events. As your body begins to relax, all the residual bodily tension that has built up during your day fades, and you may experience a twitch as the last of the tension releases. This twitch is known as the hypnic jerk and can give you the feeling of falling off an edge as you *'fall asleep'*.

Your dreaming adventures form part of your sleep cycles and, in an average night, you will experience five of these sleep cycles and so create five dream episodes. The first of these episodes will last for 10 to 15 minutes and the length of your dream episodes increases with each sleep cycle until the final episode, which can be around 40 to 45 minutes long. As you reach the end of your final sleep cycle, you pass through the threshold between dreaming and waking, known as the hypnopompic stage. You will still be creating dream imagery at this point but will be becoming more aware of your waking surroundings. This is an excellent time to practice lucid dreaming.

Lucid dreaming is the ability to realize that you are dreaming and then to consciously influence your dream without waking up. The first few times that you become aware that you are dreaming can be quite frustrating as your conscious self will probably just try to wake up. The more you practise, however, particularly during the hypnopompic stage, the more you will be able to maintain your lucidity and so influence your dreams. The most popular uses of lucid dreaming are flying to some exotic dream destination and also indulging in intimate erotic experiences, often in the same dream.

Although lucid dreaming can be enjoyed to create particularly pleasurable experiences, it can also be used to resolve more practical tensions in your waking life. Lucid dreaming will not reduce these waking stresses automatically but it will help you to understand the underlying causes of the tensions and work through them. Part of the excitement of lucid dreaming is the realization that you have the power to do anything you wish in the world you have created. By using lucid dreams to work through challenging situations in your waking life, you begin to realize that you also have the power to create the day-to-day reality that you want to live in.

Dream Substances

One of the best ways to positively influence your dreams is to take care of the types of food, drink and other substances that you accept into your body. Although we often think of dreaming as just occurring in the brain, bodily tensions and discomfort can also have an effect on your dream state. There are many misconceptions about how your diet affects your dream content and the most enduring of these fallacies is that cheese gives you nightmares. Although the food we eat can affect our dream patterns, the key factor isn't the compounds it contains but how easily your body digests it.

The more digestible a food, the more relaxed your body will be when you are asleep. Like most other fatty foods, cheese takes quite a bit of effort to digest so it causes our sleep to be restless, making us more likely to drift in and out of wakefulness. This makes us far more aware of our dream content and, because our body isn't fully relaxed, our dream content is often less than relaxing as well. Other foods, such as hot curries or anything particularly spicy, can also cause similar levels of restlessness, as will any heavy meal eaten just before you go to sleep.

Any substance that prevents your body from fully relaxing during sleep will tend to make your dreams seem more vivid and intense. The scariest of these can be the dreaded nicotine nightmares, caused by wearing a nicotine patch as you sleep. Smoking tends to reduce the intensity of your dreams and so when you give up smoking, your dreaming activity will return in incredibly vivid and realistic detail. Recent ex-smokers attempting to sleep while buzzing on slowly absorbed nicotine will have some of the wildest dreams that they can possibly imagine. To help your body rest and heal, it is best not to wear nicotine patches while you sleep.

Alcohol is a mild depressant and is commonly used as a sedative to help induce sleep. Although alcohol does make you feel more relaxed and can help you to get off to sleep, its effects soon wear off and instead of being a sedative, it becomes a stimulant. Alcohol also suppresses dreaming by inhibiting the periods of REM sleep that we all need in order to dream. If your REM sleep is temporarily inhibited, it then returns in an REM rebound where your dreams are much more vivid, scary and intense than normal. Processing alcohol also causes the body some physiological stress and this unease is often reflected in nightmarish confusion and anxiety in your dream content.

Using prescription medicines can also result in poor quality sleep and the associated intense dream experiences. Ironically, some of these drugs are sleeping pills, which are intended to promote a good night's sleep, but often result in similar experiences to alcohol, causing REM rebound and restlessness as they start to wear off during the night. Antidepressants may also cause the inhibition of REM sleep and, although this might seem a good result, as the user will have fewer nightmares, it also means that they will find it difficult to use their dreams to resolve the situations in waking life that may be causing the onset of depression.

Nightmares

Nightmares can be very scary experiences but a nightmare is just a particular type of dream experience where your emotions are heightened and a situation feels out of control. Although the nightmare may seem uncontrollable, you are creating it, and so you can also take steps to resolve it. The reason that you create a nightmare isn't to scare or upset yourself but to make yourself aware that something is out of balance in your waking life. If you try to ignore this imbalance, your unconscious awareness will begin to increase the emotional content of the dream and make it apparently scarier and scarier until you start to consciously pay attention.

The most disturbing aspect of a nightmare can be the feeling that you have no control over it. You may often feel terrified as your unconscious self illuminates some of your frustrated intentions and unresolved tensions from waking life. Although this can be a nightmarish experience, you are trying to tell yourself something of vital importance and as soon as you start paying attention to this issue, the nightmare will fade.

It can seem easier to avoid scary dreams but the gift of the nightmare is that it will help you to identify specific solutions to the frustrations and anxieties you may be experiencing in everyday life.

You can usually find the message that you are trying to communicate to yourself by understanding the content of the dream patterns in your nightmare. Many of the patterns described in this book can be experienced as nightmares and you can use these descriptions to become more aware of what is causing you to create the nightmare. This will help you to reflect more rationally on the particular situation and formulate a specific plan of action to resolve it. There is a more direct way to resolve a nightmare but it requires a little courage and self-control.

There is often a period in a nightmare where it becomes so incredibly scary that you force yourself to wake up. This is the crucial moment and your instinctive reaction is usually to remove yourself from the nightmare by wakening fully. This is the key point in dealing with the nightmare because you are so emotionally engaged with it. Instead of waking up, find the single most frightening aspect of the nightmare and confront it by asking it what it is trying to tell you. This may seem even more terrifying for a few microseconds but usually you will hear a clear and honest reply.

The answer you hear is the key to releasing the nightmare, so you can use this information to take action and resolve the tension in your waking life. Nightmares are among the most emotionally charged of dreams, and putting your answer into action may feel quite an emotional challenge. Your ability to create such powerful and emotive dream imagery, however, shows that you have the strength and power to take decisive action in your waking life. The more familiar that you become with your nightmares, the more you can influence your instincts and emotions, rather than feeling that they are controlling you.

Healing Dreams

One of the greatest gifts of a dream is that it can help you to identify tensions in your waking life and illuminate how to resolve them. These imbalances are often generated as you explore your true characteristics, actual needs and real beliefs. Although these may appear to be quite intangible, any tensions in your waking life can make you feel ill at ease, and imbalances may manifest themselves physically in the form of a *'dis-ease'* or illness. These physical tensions may be experienced as minor aches and pains or can show up as more serious illnesses, which require specific medical attention.

As well as helping to resolve imbalances that can lead to various ailments, dreams can also be used to give advance warning of impending illness. These are known as prodromal dreams, from the Greek *pro dromus* meaning *'fore runner'*. As our dream language is metaphorical, dreams of particular diseases do not usually reflect actual illnesses, so we have to look at our dream imagery for clues. For example, one of my clients had a recurring dream that some strangers were building another house in his garden without asking for his permission. This new house began to cast a shadow on his house and the building work was causing problems with the communal plumbing.

My client was also suffering from increasingly frequent urinary upsets so I suggested he go for a medical check-up as the unwanted house might represent an unwanted growth inside

his body. A superficial bladder tumour was found but there was a waiting list for the required medical procedure. As well as diagnosing illness, dreams can also be used in the healing process, and so to work with the growth until a medical appointment was available, we used a visualization process. My client was a keen ornithologist and I guided him through a visioning where he was a magnificent and powerful golden eagle, soaring in a bright sky above a wild coast.

We symbolized the tumour cells as rabbits grazing near the water's edge, apparently harmless but becoming a real nuisance as they multiplied out of control. In the visualization, his golden eagle swooped down, plucking off the rabbits one by one. After I had taken my client through this process a few times, he could do it on his own and by the time his operation date arrived, the growth had shrunk to the point where the operation was no longer required. This may have been a result of our work together, or it may have been down to a lifestyle and diet change. Either way, the dream and the visualization had given my client a powerful and healing awareness.

By using your dreams to resolve imbalances in your body, you can begin to heal yourself and make yourself whole again. Dreams and healing have always been closely intertwined and the Yellow Emperor in China first recorded use of dream healing 4,500 years ago. The originator of modern medicine, Hippocrates, often used dream interpretation as part of his diagnosis and the traditional Hippocratic Oath also refers to Asclepius, the Greek God of healing and medicine, who inspired a number of dream temples. Patients would sleep in these temples and could begin to heal themselves by using their dreams to understand how to make themselves whole again.

Your Dream Body

Although your unconscious awareness may seem to be a quality only associated with your mind, it is actually present at a physical, emotional and spiritual level, too. Beyond the more obvious sensations and physicality of your conscious body, you also have an unconsciously aware body. Even though you may feel that you are consciously aware of your body at all times and completely in control of it, your body is unconsciously gesturing, moving and speaking without you consciously realizing it. This unconscious physical awareness is your dream body and embodies all your natural and instinctive physicality.

Your dream body personifies who you truly are, what you really need and how you can actually achieve it, but you can often ignore your true self by consciously forcing your body to behave in unnatural ways. Trying to consciously control your body can cause a great deal of tension between who you really are and how you think you should appear to other people. Our bodies are living, breathing creatures and, rather than luxuriating in them, we often treat them as objects to be starved, tweaked and tucked. We tend to try and control our bodies for the reflected judgement of how we appear to others, rather than for our own satisfaction.

The most common method of body control is limiting what you actually put into your body by trying to stick to a particular diet. Your unconscious body often rebels against this strict dietary regime, however, and you may find your bodily appearance getting even more out of control. Although you think you are taking in food to provide a number of calories and satisfy a physical hunger, you are usually eating to fulfil an unspoken and unconscious need. These needs are apparent in your

dream patterns and by attending to them, your dream body will begin to form into its natural healthy physicality and shape.

If you dream about having little control or power, then you may try to control your life by regulating what you put into your body. This might involve excess eating or starving yourself, and sometimes both in a binge cycle. If you dream that something is missing from your life, then you will tend to have an appetite for comfort food, eating to make yourself feel better, rather than because you are hungry and need nourishment. Dreams of unfulfilled need often manifest in habitual eating, where you keep eating more and more, even though just physically feeding your body isn't fulfilling your emotional needs.

Understanding the meanings and messages from the patterns of your dreams will help you to positively identify your real needs and what you really value. The more you attend to your real needs and how to fulfil them, the less you will need to control yourself by restricting what you eat. The more comfortable you are in your skin, the less you will allow others to judge your appearance. It may seem as if relaxing control of your regimes and procedures will just cause your appearance to go out of control, but the reverse is true. The more you attend to your real needs, the more easily your natural and healthy dream body will emerge.

Your Dream Mind

Your mind may appear to be the one area of your body that is completely conscious but you have an older and wiser mind, which unconsciously absorbs and processes deeper thoughts, inspiring and igniting bigger ideas. This wiser mind is your dream mind and can do something that no conscious mind, however bright and clever, can do. Your conscious mind works at a rational level requiring the certainty of confirmation, while your dream mind can embrace paradox and possibility. Instead of needing to definitely have all the facts, your dream mind thrives on creating awareness just from glimpses and fragments of information.

It can be difficult to consciously make a decision when working with incomplete information but your dream mind excels at working with uncertainties and ambiguities. This quality makes your unconscious awareness more adept at stepping into the unknown and making innovative breakthroughs. Rather than logically working its way, step by step, though rational decision chains, your dream mind makes deeper sense of your world by matching patterns and making analogies. As well as the great scientific minds of Albert Einstein, Niels Bohr and Friedrich Kekulé, many others have used the brilliance of their dream minds to realize technological revelations that would have been almost impossible to achieve in any other way.

Although a computer may be the most rational and logical device imaginable, two of its originators, Charles Babbage and Ada Lovelace, used their unconscious minds to dream it up. Babbage was a mathematics professor at Cambridge University and he often related how he would allow himself to doze off as he worked at the facilities of the Analytical Society. As he dreamt, with his head leaning forward on the wooden table, his dream mind was exploring different tables. These were logarithmic tables, and his dreams enabled him to devise the Difference Engine, the forerunner of all modern computing hardware.

Ada Lovelace was an English countess who worked with Babbage on the Analytical Engine, which was a development

of the Difference Engine, and could run software applications. Lovelace suffered from fevers, and these would often give rise to intense and vivid dreams. During these dreams, she realized that numbers could be used as symbols and the Analytical Engine could manipulate these symbols in the same way the dreaming mind does. Lovelace used this insight to devise a series of calculations to run on the Analytical Engine and she is now recognized as the world's first computer programmer and software author.

Although these breakthroughs may seem like works of genius, what we call genius is very often just seeing the familiar in an unfamiliar way. Your dream mind can open up narrow-minded viewpoints, and ideas that we now accept as rational reality were once often only a dream. When dealing with a challenge, we are often advised to sleep on it and it is our dreams that are the most valuable part of our sleep. When you feel stuck on a problem, try distracting your conscious awareness and allow your dream mind to unconsciously work through a variety of solutions instead.

Your Dream Relationships

The characters you create in your dreams reflect your actual relationships with the significant people in your waking life. You generate dream characters to symbolically represent parts of yourself that you are consciously unaware of, and you do the same in waking life where you shine your unconscious characteristics on to others. People you are attracted to often reflect positive qualities you possess yourself but aren't consciously aware of having. Others who you dislike may reflect behaviours you unconsciously exhibit yourself, but that your rational self will not allow you to consciously own.

You are also unconsciously aware that you reflect the identities of other people, and you may try to hide your real characteristics, so that you might appear as powerful and beautiful as possible to others. This might seem to be an overt strategy to exert more influence over others but you are usually trying to see your beauty indirectly in the reflection of your reflection, rather than having the courage to own it directly. The possibility that you have an unspoken inner beauty might be unsettling for you and so you may try to hide it, usually by attempting to conform to some norm of conventional beauty.

When you shine your unconscious qualities on to other people, you instinctively check to see what is reflected back. As you check your reflections, you unconsciously judge what you see and, although you may think that you are passing judgement on the other person, you are actually judging some of your unconscious characteristics. If you criticize someone else for being too brash and loud, then there may be an extrovert part of your behaviour you would like to express, but refuse to recognize or own up to. It is a natural self-defence to reject your behaviours if they make you feel wrong or vulnerable.

By continuing to project your unowned characteristics on to others, however, it is easy to become stuck in relationship patterns where you play out the same stories again and again. Even though the partners in your relationships change, they are still only mirrors for the characteristics that you perhaps need to recognize and resolve in your behaviours. It can be difficult to do this in waking life, but in your dreams you can clearly see these recurring relationship patterns appearing. By understanding the characters you create in your dreams you can begin to realize who you really want to attract into your waking life.

Becoming aware of your dream relationships will not only help you with your romantic and intimate relationships, it will also make you more aware of how you connect to other people in professional and social relationships. Rather than being self-conscious about how you appear to other people, you become far more self-aware about who you really are and what you really need in a relationship. As well as giving you the opportunity to be closer to another person, one of the most valuable gifts of a relationship is that it helps you to explore your deeper self.

Your Dream Journey

Dreams about birth and death are some of the most intriguing and scary experiences we can have. These dreams of being born or dying are often unsettling, particularly if we take them literally and try to relate them to actual births and deaths in our waking lives. Our dreams about life starting and ending, however, are almost invariably about the cycles of beginnings and endings of particular situations in our day-to-day lives. These cycles can be short and transitory, like the breath that you have just taken, or longer and more enduring, like your continuing journey through life. There is always a start and an end to whatever activities we are involved in.

Almost all human cultures use the metaphor of birth to signify the start of something new and death to symbolize a transformation into the next stage of the cycle. Dreams of giving birth announce fresh beginnings or a precious idea coming to fruition. Any time you dream about a birth, you are realizing that you are about to embark on a new stage in your life's journey. Your unconscious awareness may also register the subtle physical and behavioural clues that someone has become pregnant or is about to give birth in waking life, and you may weave this information into your dream stories.

Although your dreams about birth can be joyful and celebratory, dreams of death and dying can cause upset and grief, and make you feel anxious and fearful when you wake from them. Dreams about dying, however, are very rarely about an actual death. Instead, they are reflections of fundamental transformations that are taking place in your waking life. When you dream of death you are reflecting on something significant coming to a natural end in your daily life. This can signify a major change, such as leaving an old job that you have outgrown and preparing yourself for the opportunities of a new challenge.

A death dream may also suggest that it is time to move on and do something different, as your current situation is at a dead end and you need to bring your dreams and aspirations back to life. It might be that you are about to leave the familiar territory of your home and embark on a new adventure or perhaps you feel stuck in a relationship that is no longer nourishing for you. As you transform your waking life, you often begin to have dreams about pregnancy, new births and exuberant children. In these dreams you are rejoicing that you have left an old life behind in order to welcome and embrace the new.

The births and deaths you experience in your dreams also draw your attention to the journeys that you make between the starts and finishes of significant events in your waking life, and the renewing periods between all your endings and beginnings. The more aware you are of the journey that you are currently on, the easier it is to see where you have come from and where you might be going. Rather than focusing on the sorrow of what might have been and the fear of what might never be,

About Dreaming

you can begin to appreciate your bigger journey and how it can take you closer to living your dream.

Your Dream Life

In my career as a dream psychologist, I have been fortunate to work with many clients who appear to be extremely successful. To the casual observer, these people seem to have everything that could possibly be wished for, with all the fame and fortune that accompanies such achievement. Behind all the glitz and glamour, however, many of these apparently successful people suffer from depression and despondency. As we explore their dreams, we find that the people in their dreams are quite different from their real-life public characters and personas. Again and again I hear my clients saying things like *'It pays the bills, but it's just not me'* or *'Somehow, I've lost myself along the way somewhere'*.

The same thing happens to the rest of us in our less public and more conventional lives. We start off with great hopes of what we want to be and aspirations about the wonderful people who will become our companions in this great adventure. We dream of the wealth we will acquire and the stories we will tell about the great deeds that we've accomplished. A few years later, however, we are asking ourselves questions such as *'Why am I doing this job?' 'What is the meaning in what I do every day?'* and *'Why do I cause myself pain and unhappiness?'*

We all have our unique life stories, which we live out in our day-to-day realities, but we also all carry an idealized picture of how we think our lives should really be. This personal vision of a perfect life is often known as *'living the dream'* but no matter how hard we work and how much we sacrifice, these dream lives may always seem just out of reach. But the surest and most direct route to achieving your dream life is to recognize that what happens inside your unconscious awareness will often manifest in your outside reality.

By understanding the night-time dreams you unconsciously generate, you will start to hear the real story of the person you truly are and where you yearn to go in life, and you will clarify the most direct path to reach your goals. This will provide you with a deep level of self-awareness, which reveals how you can start connecting your idealized dream future with the reality of your current life. It can often be surprising to realize how close you are to connecting to some of your biggest dreams and it often only requires a decisive commitment or a change of perspective to bring them into your waking reality.

As the stories of your waking life begin converging with your dream stories, you will find yourself beginning to live your dream. If you try to hide from your dreams, they will keep searching for you until you truly find your self and can at last speak your clear truths. As your dreams discover you, you will begin to realize that you don't really have to live 'the' dream, being offered up in colour supplements and TV adverts, in order to be truly happy. Instead, you are living and breathing your dream, the one unique, big dream that only you can dream.

Living Your Dreams

When we dream, millions of years of evolution meet the minute-by-minute minutiae of our everyday lives. We have evolved into dreaming creatures; beings that don't just have the experience of one lifetime but have the distilled awareness of past generations and know of the possibilities of future ones.

Our dreams take us to the edge of what we know, illuminating all our opportunities and witnessing all our achievements. They are the greatest gifts we have and invite us to step into the mystery of who we really are, where we are going, and how we will get there.

We dream to remember who we really are and to understand the person we can become. We dream to reconnect with all the talents and ideas we possess but that we tend to neglect and ignore. We dream to play around with our potential futures and possibilities. Our dreams collect and connect all the remembered fragments of what we have experienced and what we hope to experience, and weave all those memories and hopes into a meaningful story. By understanding the stories that we create in our dreams, we can start to comprehend our uniqueness and celebrate our talents.

Living your dreams can't be accomplished by just being an impartial observer, evaluating your situation from a distance. Stepping fully into your dreams is the only real way to meet the person who you dream of being, and to truly live your dreams you have to allow yourself to become immersed in your wider awareness. Your unconscious awareness is continually trying to connect you with your dream self, the bigger self beyond your conscious self, but it can be easy to ignore it. The more that you connect with the world beyond yourself, however, the more profoundly you will connect with your own deeper self.

All our relationships, spiritual practices and art that we create are driven by our desire to transcend our mere physicality by connecting with something beyond ourselves. Our greatest accomplishments as humans have started with just the glimpse of a dream of how things could be. It can be easy to dismiss our dreaming as being inconsequential and random flickering in the electric oceans of our brains, but being aware of our dreams and turning them into an actual reality is the essence of being human. Our dreams connect us all and, as we sleep, we create worlds that we all recognize.

As you read these words, your unconscious awareness is quietly working away in the background, naturally lighting up some of the 100 billion neurons that collectively form your brain. Many of these individual neurons may appear to be firing quite randomly without any deeper purpose but their coordinated activity accumulates into something much more meaningful. Every single one of your brain cells instinctively connects with other neurons beyond, allowing familiar themes and patterns to emerge from the thousands of connections they make. Your dreams are the stories of all those connections that you create and all the possibilities they illuminate for you.

Hay House Titles of Related Interest

The Dream Whisperer,
by Davina Mackail

Dreams and Beyond,
by Madhu Tandan

The Hidden Power of Dreams,
by Denise Linn

A Stream of Dreams,
by Leon Nacson

WIN a Dream Interpretation
with Ian Wallace

Have you ever had a recurring dream or puzzled over what a dream means to you?

If so, then this is your chance to have your dream interpreted by one of the world's leading dream experts.

Ian Wallace is a dream psychologist and has analysed over 100,000 dreams for his clients. He is regularly on the Steve Wright and Chris Evans shows, and is celebrated for his accuracy. Hay House are offering one lucky person the chance to win a one-to-one dream interpretation with Ian. The winner will have their chosen dream interpreted by Ian over the phone.

To enter the competition all you need to do is answer the following question and visit www.hayhouse.co.uk/dream-interpretation to submit your answer. Closing date for entries is 31st December 2011.

Q. Who is the author of *The Top 100 Dreams*?

Terms and Conditions

The competition is for one winner to win a dream interpretation over the phone with Ian Wallace. By entering the competition you will automatically join the Hay House mailing list to receive news about our upcoming releases and events. No multiple entries allowed. All entrants must be aged 18 or over. All entries must be received by 31st December 2011. The competition winner will be informed by 9th January 2012. Prize must be claimed within six months of the winner being notified.

ABOUT THE AUTHOR

Ian Wallace is a qualified psychologist who specialises in dreams and dreaming. He regularly appears on television and radio, and in print, where he is consistently acknowledged for his articulacy, accuracy and authority. Ian has an encyclopaedic knowledge of dreams and the dreaming process based on his analysis of over 100,000 dreams, and has more than 30 years of experience putting his learning into successful practice. He has a solid academic grounding in the theoretical psychology of dreaming and the unique ability to articulate these complex psychological principles in a very straightforward and engaging manner. This brings the dreaming experience to life, so the dreamer can really own the dream and take practical action with the messages that it reveals.

As well as working with his individual clients, many of whom are household names, Ian works with larger groups and blue-chip corporations. He is the founder of the Dream Organisation, which helps businesses connect with their true purpose and potential by making tangible sense of their possible futures. Ian's role ranges from delivering keynotes to facilitating workshops and leading immersive group experiences. The revolutionary work done by the Dream Organisation is based on the Archegyre. This is a model of human behaviour, created by Ian, that describes all aspects of human experience and encompasses a span of awareness reaching all the way from ancient wisdom through to contemporary psychological research.

www.ianwallacedreams.com